Messages from
The Universal House of Justice
1968~1973

Messages from
The Universal House of Justice
1968-1973

BAHÁ'Í PUBLISHING TRUST • WILMETTE, ILLINOIS

Library of Congress Cataloging in Publication Data

Universal House of Justice.
  Messages from the Universal House of Justice,
1968-1973.

  Includes index.
  1. Bahaism—Addresses, essays, lectures.
BP375,U54 1975   297'.89   75-11795
ISBN 0-87743-076-4
ISBN 0-87743-096-9 pbk.

Printed in United States of America

Contents

Foreword

This volume is a sequel to *Wellspring of Guidance* which was published in 1969. It comprises communications from The Universal House of Justice spanning the period of that institution's second five-year term, Riḍván 1968 to Riḍván 1973. Beginning with the announcement of the results of the election at the second International Convention, this collection of selected messages portrays Bahá'í developments during the latter half of the Nine Year Plan in addition to conveying the guidance, advice, and comments of The House of Justice on a variety of questions confronting the Bahá'í world community at various stages of the Plan.

The establishment of the Continental Boards of Counselors, the commemorations of the centenary of Bahá'u'lláh's arrival in the Holy Land, of the fiftieth anniversary of 'Abdu'l-Bahá's passing and of the centenary of the martyrdom of the Purest Branch, the completion of the synopsis and codification of the Kitáb-i-Aqdas, the adoption of the Constitution of The Universal House of Justice, the purchase of the Mazra'ih Mansion, the dedication of the Panama Temple, the holding of a series of eight continental and oceanic conferences between August 1970 and September 1971, the decision to build the seat of The Universal House of Justice, the attainment of consultative status with the Economic and Social Council of the United Nations—all indelible landmarks of the Nine Year Plan—are treated in this volume.

In general, the messages are addressed to the Bahá'ís of the world, to National Spiritual Assemblies, or to believers gathered at special events. Two messages are addressed jointly to Continental Boards of Counselors and National Spiritual Assemblies. One is addressed to Bahá'í youth in every land. A letter to an individual, appearing under the title "Comments on the Guardianship and The Universal House of Justice," is included because of the general interest of its subject matter to all Bahá'ís.

The reader will readily observe some differences in the presentation of the book's contents: The messages have been printed as complete documents and therefore include addressees, salutations, and complimentary closes as in the originals. A subject heading has been provided for each communication by the editors but subheadings have not been inserted as has been the practice in the past. Several items have been extracted from *Wellspring of Guidance* to make this volume chronologically complete.

Except for three messsages, all these communications have appeared in part or in whole in the various Bahá'í journals. It is, therefore, for the easier reference and greater use of the Bahá'í community that they are now gathered in this anthology.

NATIONAL SPIRITUAL ASSEMBLY OF
THE BAHÁ'ÍS OF THE UNITED STATES

Messages from
The Universal House of Justice
1968-1973

Election of
The Universal House of Justice—Riḍván 1968

22 April 1968

To All National Spiritual Assemblies

Dear Bahá'í Friends,

The following cable has been sent to the National Spiritual Assembly of the Baháís of the United States for publication in "Baháí News":

Announce Baháí world newly elected members Universal House of Justice Amoz Gibson 'Alí Na<u>kh</u>javání Hushmand Fatheázam Ian Semple Charles Wolcott David Hofman H. Borrah Kavelin Hugh Chance David Ruhe.

With loving Baháí greetings,
THE UNIVERSAL HOUSE OF JUSTICE

Message to National Conventions 1968

9 May 1968

To the National Spiritual Assembly of the
Baháís of the United States,

Beloved Friends,

The following message is being sent to National Conventions. It is in the form of a cable since it was necessary to send it as such to some National Spiritual Assemblies because of the

3

time element. Please convey it to the friends assembled at your Convention:

> With joyful memory of dedicated spirit mature deliberations Second International Convention hail golden opportunity national conventions as crucial midway point Nine Year Plan approaches galvanize believers direct all efforts achievement every remaining goal and simultaneously extend accelerate universal proclamation divine message. With utmost love call upon all Bahá'ís for sacrificial outpouring energies resources advancement redeeming order Bahá'u'lláh sole refuge misdirected heedless millions. World Center Faith scene prolonged prayerful consultation with assembled Hands Cause goals Plan including fundamental objective development institution Hands view extension future Godgiven duties protection propagation. Supplicating continually Holy Shrines Lord Hosts bountifully reward dedicated ardent lovers complete glorious victory.
>
> With loving Bahá'í greetings,
THE UNIVERSAL HOUSE OF JUSTICE

Establishment of Eleven
Continental Boards of Counselors

21 June 1968

To: All National Spiritual Assemblies

Dear Bahá'í Friends,

The following cable has today been sent to the National Spiritual Assembly of the Bahá'ís of the United States for publication in "Bahá'í News":

> Rejoice announce momentous decision establish eleven Continental Boards Counselors protection propagation

Faith three each for Africa Americas Asia one each for Australasia Europe. Adoption this significant step following consultation with Hands Cause God ensures extension future appointed functions their institution. Continental Boards entrusted in close collaboration Hands Cause with responsibility direction Auxiliary Boards and consultation National Spiritual Assemblies. Hands Cause God will henceforth increase intercontinental services assuming worldwide role protection propagation Faith. Members Auxiliary Boards will report be responsible to Continental Boards Counselors. Hands Cause residing Holy Land in addition serving liaison between Universal House Justice and Continental Boards Counselors will assist future establishment International Teaching Center Holy Land foreshadowed writings beloved Guardian. Details new developments being conveyed by letter. Fervently supplicating Holy Threshold divine confirmations further step irresistible unfoldment mighty Administrative Order Bahá'u'lláh (Signed) Universal House of Justice.

> With loving Bahá'í greetings,
> THE UNIVERSAL HOUSE OF JUSTICE

Appointment of Continental Boards of Counselors

24 June 1968

To the Bahá'ís of the World

Dear Bahá'í Friends,

The majestic unfoldment of Bahá'u'lláh's world-redeeming administrative system has been marked by the successive establishment of the various institutions and agencies which constitute the framework of that divinely-created Order. Thus, more than a quarter-of-a-century after the emergence of the first National Spiritual Assemblies of the Bahá'í world the Institution of the Hands of the Cause of God was formally established, with the appointment by the beloved Guardian, in conformity with the provisions of 'Abdu'l-Bahá's Will and Testament, of the first contingent of these high-ranking officers of the Faith. Following the passing of the Guardian of the Cause of God, it fell to the House of Justice to devise a way, within the Administrative Order, of developing "the Institution of the Hands of the Cause with a view to extension into the future of its appointed functions of protection and propagation," and this was made a goal of the Nine Year Plan. Much thought and study has been given to the question over the past four years, and the texts have been collected and reviewed. During the last two months, this goal, as announced in our cable to the National Conventions, has been the object of prolonged and prayerful consultation between the Universal House of Justice and the Hands of the Cause of God. All this made evident the framework within which this goal was to be achieved, namely:

> The Universal House of Justice sees no way in which additional Hands of the Cause of God can be appointed.

> The absence of the Guardian of the Faith brought about an entirely new relationship between the Universal House of Justice and the Hands of the Cause and called for the progressive unfoldment by the Universal House of Justice of the manner in which the Hands of the Cause would carry out their divinely-conferred functions of protection and propagation.

> Whatever new development or institution is initiated should come into operation as soon as possible in order to reinforce and supplement the work of the Hands of the Cause while at the same time taking full advantage of the

opportunity of having the Hands themselves assist in launching and guiding the new procedures.

Any such institution must grow and operate in harmony with the principles governing the functioning of the Institution of the Hands of the Cause of God.

In the light of these considerations the Universal House of Justice decided, as announced in its recent cable, to establish Continental Boards of Counselors for the protection and propagation of the Faith. Their duties will include directing the Auxiliary Boards in their respective areas, consulting and collaborating with National Spiritual Assemblies, and keeping the Hands of the Cause and the Universal House of Justice informed concerning the conditions of the Cause in their areas.

Initially eleven Boards of Counselors have been appointed, one for each of the following areas: Northwestern Africa, Central and East Africa, Southern Africa, North America, Central America, South America, Western Asia, Southeastern Asia, Northeastern Asia, Australasia and Europe.

The members of these Boards of Counselors will serve for a term, or terms, the length of which will be determined and announced at a later date, and while serving in this capacity, will not be eligible for membership on national or local administrative bodies. One member of each Continental Board of Counselors has been designated as Trustee of the Continental Fund for its area.

The Auxiliary Boards for Protection and Propagation will henceforth report to the Continental Boards of Counselors who will appoint or replace members of the Auxiliary Boards as circumstances may require. Such appointments and replacements as may be necessary in the initial stages will take place after consultation with the Hand or Hands previously assigned to the continent or zone.

The Hands of the Cause of God have the prerogative and

obligation to consult with the Continental Boards of Counselors and National Spiritual Assemblies on any subject which, in their view, affects the interests of the Cause. The Hands residing in the Holy Land will act as liaison between the Universal House of Justice and the Continental Boards of Counselors, and will also assist the Universal House of Justice in setting up, at a propitious time, an international teaching center in the Holy Land, as anticipated in the Guardian's writings.

The Hands of the Cause of God are one of the most precious assets the Bahá'í world possesses. Released from administration of the Auxiliary Boards, they will be able to concentrate their energies on the more primary responsibilities of general protection and propagation, "preservation of the spiritual health of the Bahá'í communities" and "the vitality of the faith" of the Bahá'ís throughout the world. The House of Justice will call upon them to undertake special missions on its behalf, to represent it on both Bahá'í and other occasions and to keep it informed of the welfare of the Cause. While the Hands of the Cause will, naturally, have special concern for the affairs of the Cause in the areas in which they reside, they will operate increasingly on an intercontinental level, a factor which will lend tremendous impetus to the diffusion throughout the Bahá'í world of the spiritual inspiration channeled through them—the Chief Stewards of Bahá'u'lláh's embryonic World Commonwealth.

With joyful hearts we proclaim this further unfoldment of the Administrative Order of Bahá'u'lláh and join our prayers to those of the friends throughout the East and the West that Bahá'u'lláh may continue to shower His confirmations upon the efforts of His servants in the safeguarding and promotion of His Faith.

With loving Bahá'í greetings,
THE UNIVERSAL HOUSE OF JUSTICE

First Appointments to
Continental Boards of Counselors

24 June 1968

To: All National Spiritual Assemblies

Dear Bahá'í Friends,

We list below the names of those who have been appointed to the first Continental Boards of Counselors for the Protection and Propagation of the Faith:

Northwestern Africa
> Ḥusayn Ardikání (Trustee, Continental Fund), Muḥammad Kebdani, William Maxwell.

Central and East Africa
> Oloro Epyeru, Kolonario Oule, Isobel Sabri, Mihdí Samandarí, 'Azíz Yazdí (Trustee, Continental Fund).

Southern Africa
> Seewoosumbur-Jeehoba Appa, Shidán Fatḥ-i-A'ẓam (Trustee, Continental Fund), Bahíyyih Ford.

North America
> Lloyd Gardiner, Florence Mayberry, Edna True (Trustee, Continental Fund).

Central America
> Carmen de Burafato, Artemus Lamb, Alfred Osborne (Trustee, Continental Fund).

South America
> Athos Costas, Hooper Dunbar (Trustee, Continental Fund), Donald Witzel.

Western Asia
> Masíḥ Farhangí, Mas'úd Khamsí, Hádí Raḥmání (Trustee, Continental Fund), Manúchihr Salmánpúr, Sankaran-Nair Vasudevan.

Southeast Asia
> Yan Kee Leong, Khudárahm Paymán (Trustee, Continental Fund), Chellie Sundram.

Northeast Asia
   Rúḥu'lláh Mumtází (Trustee, Continental Fund), Vicente
      Samaniego.
Australasia
   Suhayl 'Alá'í, Howard Harwood, Thelma Perks (Trustee,
      Continental Fund).
Europe
   Erik Blumenthal, Dorothy Ferraby (Trustee, Continental
      Fund), Louis Hénuzet.

Please share this list with the friends.

> With loving Bahá'í greetings
> The Universal House of Justice

Message to the First Oceanic Conference

August 1968

To the Hands of the Cause of God
   and the Bahá'í Friends Assembled in Palermo, Sicily
   at the First Bahá'í Oceanic Conference.

Dearly-loved Friends,

   The event which we commemorate at this first Bahá'í
Oceanic Conference is unique. Neither the migration of
Abraham from Ur of the Chaldees to the region of Aleppo, nor
the journey of Moses towards the Promised Land, nor the
flight into Egypt of Mary and Joseph with the infant Jesus, nor
yet the Hegira of Muḥammad can compare with the voyage
made by God's Supreme Manifestation one hundred years ago
from Gallipoli to the Most Great Prison. Bahá'u'lláh's voyage
was forced upon Him by the two despots who were His chief
adversaries in a determined attempt to extirpate once and for
all His Cause, and the decree of His fourth banishment came
when the tide of His prophetic utterance was in full flood. The
proclamation of His Message to mankind had begun; the sun

of His majesty had reached its zenith and, as attested by the devotion of His followers, the respect of the population and the esteem of officials and the representatives of foreign powers, His ascendancy had become manifest. At such a time He was confronted with the decree of final exile to a remote, obscure and pestilential outpost of the decrepit Turkish empire.

Bahá'u'lláh knew, better than His royal persecutors, the magnitude of the crisis, with all its potentiality for disaster, which confronted Him. Consigned to a prison cell, debarred from access to those to whom His Message must be addressed, cut off from His followers save for the handful who were to accompany Him, and deprived even of association with them, it was apparent that by all earthly standards the ship of His Cause must founder, His mission wither and die.

But it was the Lord of Hosts with Whom they were dealing. Knowing the sufferings which faced Him His one thought was to instill confidence and fortitude into His followers, to whom He immediately dispatched sublime Tablets asserting the power of His Cause to overcome all opposition. "Should they attempt to conceal its light on the continent," is one of His powerful utterances on this theme, "it will assuredly rear its head in the midmost heart of the ocean, and, raising its voice, proclaim: 'I am the lifegiver of the world!' " All the afflictions which men could heap upon Him were thrown back from the rock of His adamantine will like spray from the ocean. His patient submission to the affronts of men, His fortitude, His divine genius transformed the somber notes of disaster into the diapason of triumph. At the nadir of His worldly fortunes He raised His standard of victory above the Prison City and poured forth upon mankind the healing balm of His laws and ordinances revealed in His Most Holy Book. "Until our time," comments 'Abdu'l-Bahá, "no such thing has ever occurred."

Contemplating this awe-inspiring, supernal episode, we may obtain a clearer understanding of our own times, a more confident view of their outcome and a deeper apprehension of the part we are called upon to play. That the violent disruption which has seized the entire planet is beyond the ability of men to assuage, unaided by God's revelation, is a truth repeatedly and forcibly set forth in our Writings. The old order cannot be repaired; it is being rolled up before our eyes. The moral decay and disorder convulsing human society must run their course; we can neither arrest nor divert them.

Our task is to build the Order of Bahá'u'lláh. Undeflected by the desperate expedients of those who seek to subdue the storm convulsing human life by political, economic, social or educational programs, let us, with single-minded devotion and concentrating all our efforts on our objective, raise His Divine System and sheltered within its impregnable stronghold, safe from the darts of doubtfulness, demonstrate the Bahá'í way of life. Wherever a Bahá'í community exists, whether large or small, let it be distinguished for its abiding sense of security and faith, its high standard of rectitude, its complete freedom from all forms of prejudice, the spirit of love among its members and for the closely knit fabric of its social life. The acute distinction between this and present day society will inevitably arouse the interest of the more enlightened, and as the world's gloom deepens the light of Bahá'í life will shine brighter and brighter until its brilliance must eventually attract the disillusioned masses and cause them to enter the haven of the Covenant of Bahá'u'lláh, Who alone can bring them peace and justice and an ordered life.

The great sea, on one of whose chief islands you are now gathered, within whose hinterland and islands have flourished the Jewish, the Christian and Islamic civilizations is a befitting scene for the first Oceanic Bahá'í Conference. Two millenniums ago, in this arena, the disciples of Christ performed such deeds of heroism and self-sacrifice as are remembered to this day and are forever enshrined in the annals of His Cause. A thousand years later the lands bordering the southern and western shores of this sea witnessed the glory of Islám's Golden Age.

In the day of the Promised One this same sea achieved eternal fame through its association with the Heroic and Formative Ages of His Cause. It bore upon its bosom the King of kings Himself; the Center of His Covenant crossed and recrossed it in the course of His epoch-making journeys to the West, during which He left the indelible imprint of His presence upon European and African lands; the Sign of God on earth frequently journeyed upon it. It enshrines within its depths the mortal remains of the Hand of the Cause of God Dorothy Baker and around its shores lies the dust of apostles, martyrs and pioneers. Forty-six Knights of Bahá'u'lláh are identified with seven of its islands and five of its territories. Through such and many other episodes, Mediterranean lands—ancient home of civilizations—have been endowed with spiritual potentiality to dissolve the encrustations of those once glorious but now moribund social orders and to radiate once again the light of Divine guidance.

Through dedicated, heroic and sacrificial deeds during the course of the beloved Guardian's ministry, the Faith of Bahá'u'lláh was established in this area. Eight pillars of the Universal House of Justice were raised, the first of an even larger number to be established now and during the course of future plans, to include, as envisioned by Shoghi Effendi, National Spiritual Assemblies in major islands of that historic sea.

The timing of such exciting developments is dependent upon the outcome of the Nine Year Plan. At this midway point of that Plan, although great strides have been made, more than half the goals are still to be won. The greatest deficiencies are in the opening of new centers where Bahá'ís reside and the formation of Local Spiritual Assemblies, which inevitably affects the ability to establish National Spiritual Assemblies. A dramatic upsurge of teaching—effective teaching—is necessary to make up the leeway; pioneers are needed, teachers must travel, funds must be provided. It is our hope that there will be engendered at this Conference, through your enthusiasm, prayers and spirit of devotion, a great spiritual dynamic to reinforce that grand momentum which, mounting steadily during the next four years, must carry the community of the Most Great Name to overwhelming victory in 1973.

Dear friends, within a few short days the observance of the Centenary of Bahá'u'lláh's arrival in the Holy Land will take place. The hearts and minds of the entire Bahá'í world will be focused on the Most Holy Shrine, where those privileged to attend this commemoration will circumambulate that Holy Spot and raise their prayers to the Lord of the Age. Let them remember their fellow-believers at home and supplicate from the depths of their souls for such bounties and favors to descend upon the friends of God everywhere as to cause them to rise as one man to demonstrate their love for Him Who suffered for them, by such deeds of sacrifice and devotion as shall outshine the deeds of the past and sweep away every obstacle from the onward march of the Cause of God.

With loving Bahá'í greetings,
THE UNIVERSAL HOUSE OF JUSTICE

Progress of the Nine Year Plan in the United States

14 August 1968

National Spiritual Assembly of the
Bahá'ís of the United States.

Dear Bahá'í Friends,

The number and character of achievements of your community since the Nine Year Plan was launched must indeed compel our gratitude. On the homefront, 52 Local Spiritual Assemblies have been formed and 500 new centers have been established. Traveling teachers and pioneers have gone forth from your community in troops, offering all of their resources and their very lives to the Cause. They have scattered to the far-flung fields of the globe to proclaim the glory of God's Revelation; have opened the Turks and Caicos Islands; poured into the Caribbean area carrying the torch of the Faith to new outposts there, and so firmly established the Cause in that chain of islands that a new pillar on which the Universal House of Justice rests was erected. With unfailing generosity, you have assisted your sister communities to acquire Bahá'í properties. Your community has indeed merited the title of "torch-bearers."

In view of the tasks which remain to be achieved, it is evident as we rapidly approach the midway point in the Plan, that your community now faces a challenge of colossal magnitude, for the pace of the work must be greatly accelerated if all the goals are to be won. On the homefront, 206 Local Spiritual Assemblies must be formed, including at least one in each of the four States where there has as yet been only one established, two in Puerto Rico, and the Assembly in Key West must be reestablished. No less than 787 new centers must be opened to the Faith. Abroad, pioneers and traveling teachers are still needed on every front to continue to carry the Faith forward throughout the entire world. You are called upon for further financial contributions to acquire the remaining properties so urgently needed by your sister communities. A gigantic, collective effort will be required to successfully discharge all these responsibilities.

We think it is important that you phase out the remaining homefront goals of the Nine Year Plan, adopting subsidiary plans for each year between now and Riḍván, 1973, bearing in mind the need to consolidate all the goals thus far won. When formulating plans for a consolidation program, to be carried out concurrently with the proclamation of the Faith, particular thought shold be given to the twelve States where there is now a minimum of only two Local Spiritual Assemblies.

Above all, the duty of deepening the spiritual life of your newly-enrolled co-workers is paramount, for the fate of the entire community depends upon the individual believers. Without the wholehearted support of each and every one of the friends, every measure adopted, no matter how well thought out, is foredoomed to failure. It is the individual believers who must maintain the Local Assemblies and the centers already won at the cost of such great sacrifice. It is they who must, afire with the love of Bahá'u'lláh, go forth to further broaden the base of administrative activity by forming new Assemblies and implanting the standard of Bahá'u'lláh in new localities; who must arise in response to the call to travel to the remote outposts of the Faith and push back the frontiers; and who must, through your wise and loving guidance, become your collaborators in carrying out your God-given mission.

We are deeply cognizant of the tremendous burden of responsibility you carry, but we are confident that your dearly-loved ommunity will arise with a renewed spirit to assume its weighty responsibilities.

We shall offer a special prayer for your Assembly that you will be enabled to carry forward unremittingly all your tasks to their triumphant conclusion.

> With loving Bahá'í greetings,
> THE UNIVERSAL HOUSE OF JUSTICE

Results of the Palermo Conference

8 September 1968

To: The Bahá'ís of the World

Dear Bahá'í Friends,

The glorious Conference in Palermo concluded with a burst of eager enthusiasm of determined and dedicated believers who have pledged to do their part in winning the remaining goals of the Nine Year Plan. More than 125 offered to pioneer and more than 100 volunteered to do travel teaching. In addition, there was a generous outpouring of material resources to finance teaching projects. Had the entire Bahá'í world been able to participate in the Mediterranean Conference we have no doubt that all the goals would be quickly won.

With this in mind we wish to impress upon the friends who could not attend the Conference, and who will surely —through reports and personal contact with those who did —sense the enthusiasm generated there, that all believers have the privilege to share in the pioneering work, in the travel teaching program and in contributing to the Fund.

We announced at the Conference that the International Deputization Fund, so far used to aid pioneering and travel teaching on an international level, will henceforth be available to assist such projects on the national level in those areas where support is vitally important to the winning of the goals of the Nine Year Plan. We are concerned that, although we are now approaching the midway point of the Plan we must yet form an additional 6,997 Local Spiritual Assemblies (76% of the goal), and take the Faith to over 22,800 new localities (59% of the goal). Obviously, hundreds of pioneers and traveling teachers will be required, many of whom will serve in their own countries.

Those who cannot pioneer or do travel teaching will want to participate by contributing to the International Deputization Fund. Let them remember Bahá'u'lláh's injunction: "Center your energies in the propagation of the Faith of God. Whoso is worthy of so high a calling, let him arise and promote it. Whoso is unable, it is his duty to appoint him who will, in his stead, proclaim this Revelation . . ." Let the Bahá'ís of the world join in the true spirit of universal participation and win all the victories while there is yet time. Let each assume his full measure of responsibility that all may share the laurels of accomplishment at the end of the Plan.

Our fervent prayer is that this one-hundredth anniversary of the final banishment of Bahá'u'lláh will mark a significant turning point in the fortunes of the Nine Year Plan.

> With loving Bahá'í greetings,
> THE UNIVERSAL HOUSE OF JUSTICE

Advice to Bahá'í Youth
Concerning Pioneering and Education

9 October 1968

To the Bahá'í Youth in Every Land

Dear Bahá'í Friends,

In the two years since we last addressed the youth of the Bahá'í world many remarkable advances have been made in the fortunes of the Faith. Not the least of these is the enrollment under the banner of Bahá'u'lláh of a growing army of young men and women eager to serve His Cause. The zeal, the enthusiasm, the steadfastness and the devotion of the youth in every land has brought great joy and assurance to our hearts.

During the last days of August and the first days of September, when nearly two thousand believers from all over the world gathered in the Holy Land to commemorate the Centenary of Bahá'u'lláh's arrival on these sacred shores, we had an opportunity to observe at first hand those qualities of good character, selfless service and determined effort exemplified in the youth who served as volunteer helpers, and we wish to express our gratitude for their loving assistance and for their example.

Many of them offered to pioneer, but one perplexing question recurred: Shall I continue my education, or should I pioneer now? Undoubtedly this same question is in the mind of every young Bahá'í wishing to dedicate his life to the advancement of the Faith. There is no stock answer which applies to all situations; the beloved Guardian gave different answers to different individuals on this question. Obviously circumstances vary with each individual case. Each individual must decide how he can best serve the Cause. In making this decision, it will be helpful to weigh the following factors:

> Upon becoming a Bahá'í one's whole life is, or should become devoted to the progress of the Cause of God, and every talent or faculty he possesses is ultimately committed to this overriding life objective. Within this framework he must consider, among other things, whether by continuing his education now he can be a more effective pioneer later, or alternatively whether the urgent need for pioneers, while possibilities for teaching are still open, outweighs an anticipated increase in effectiveness. This is not an easy decision, since oftentimes the spirit which prompts the pioneering offer is more important than one's academic attainments.

> One's liability for military service may be a factor in timing the offer of pioneer service.

> One may have outstanding obligations to others, including those who may be dependent on him for support.

> It may be possible to combine a pioneer project with a continuing educational program. Consideration may also be given to the possibility that a pioneering experience, even though it interrupts the formal educational program, may prove beneficial in the long run in that studies would later be resumed with a more mature outlook.

> The urgency of a particular goal which one is especially qualified to fill and for which there are no other offers.

> The fact that the need for pioneers will undoubtedly be with

us for many generations to come, and that therefore there will be many calls in future for pioneering service.

The principle of consultation also applies. One may have the obligation to consult others, such as one's parents, one's Local and National Assemblies, and the pioneering committees.

Finally, bearing in mind the principle of sacrificial service and the unfailing promises Bahá'u'lláh ordained for those who arise to serve His Cause, one should pray and meditate on what his course of action will be. Indeed, it often happens that the answer will be found in no other way.

We assure the youth that we are mindful of the many important decisions they must make as they tread the path of service to Bahá'u'lláh. We will offer our ardent supplications at the Holy Threshold that all will be divinely guided and that they will attract the blessings of the All-Merciful.

> Deepest Bahá'í love,
> THE UNIVERSAL HOUSE OF JUSTICE

Riḍván Message 1969

Riḍván 126 [1969]

To the Bahá'ís of the World.

Dearly-loved Friends,

The continued progress of the Cause of God stands in vivid contrast to the chronic unrest afflicting human society, a contrast which the events of the past year, both within and without the Faith, have only served to intensify. Amidst the disintegration of the old order the Cause of God has pursued its majestic course, extending the range of its activities and influence and accomplishing a further development of its administrative system.

Opening with the convening, in the Holy Land, of the Second International Convention for the election of the Universal House of Justice, the year has witnessed a remarkable activity in the Cause. The most significant and far-reaching development was undoubtedly the appointment of the eleven Continental Boards of Counselors, which fulfilled the goal of the Nine Year Plan calling for the development of the Institution of the Hands of the Cause of God with a view to the extension into the future of its appointed functions of protection and propagation. This step, taken after full consultation with the Hands of the Cause, has, at one and the same time, strongly reinforced the activities of that Institution and made it possible for the Hands themselves to extend the range of their individual services beyond the continental sphere, thereby making universally available to the friends the love, the wisdom and the spirit of dedication animating the Guardian's appointees. We wish to pay tribute at this time to the exemplary manner in which the Counselors, under the guidance of the Hands, have embarked upon their high duties.

In August, the first Oceanic Bahá'í Conference, held in Palermo, commemorated Bahá'u'lláh's voyage on the Mediterranean Sea on His way to the Most Great Prison. Attendants at this Conference came immediately afterwards to the Qiblih of their Faith to pay homage at the Shrine of its Founder and to commemorate with deep awareness of its spiritual import the long prophesied arrival of the Lord of Hosts on the shores of the Holy Land. This gathering of more than two thousand believers presented an inexpressibly poignant contrast to the actual arrival of Bahá'u'lláh one hundred years before, rejected by the rulers of this earth and derided by the local populace. Such is the conquering power of His Message, such is the undefeatable might of the King of Kings.

That same Message is now being proclaimed by His followers from end to end of the world. Already one hundred and twenty-two Heads of State have been presented with the special edition of "The Proclamation of Bahá'u'lláh," and copies have been received by thousands more officials and leaders.

Taking full advantage of the designation of 1968 as Human Rights Year by the United Nations, Bahá'í communities throughout the world have not only strengthened the ties between the Bahá'í International Community and the United Nations, but have at the same time proclaimed the Faith and its healing message. In country after country the Cause has been featured for the first time in modern mass communications media. The volume of this call to the peoples of the world is increasing day by day and must so continue, penetrating every stratum of society, until the conclusion of the Plan and beyond.

As a stimulus and aid to this vital work as well as to the promotion of all the goals of the Plan, we announce the holding between August 1970 and September 1971 of a series of eight Oceanic and Continental Conferences, as follows: La Paz, Bolivia, and Rose Hill, Mauritius, in August 1970; Monrovia, Liberia, and Djakarta, Indonesia, in January 1971; Suva, Fiji, and Kingston, Jamaica, in May 1971; Sapporo, Japan, and Reykjavik, Iceland, in September 1971.

A review of the progress of the Nine Year Plan discloses that great strides have been made in the acquisition of Ḥaẓíratu'l-Quds, Temple sites and Teaching Institutes, in translation of Bahá'í literature into more languages and in the incorporation of Local and National Spiritual Assemblies. The site of the Panama Temple has been prepared for construction which will begin as soon as final plans and specifications and the placing of the contract have been approved.

As a result of the accelerated pace of expansion and consolidation which has been initiated, and which, if fostered and fed, will become a full tide of victorious achievement, we joyfully announce the formation of twelve more National

Spiritual Assemblies, two during Riḍván 1969: the National Spiritual Assembly of the Bahá'ís of Burundi and Rwanda with its seat in Bujumbura and the National Spiritual Assembly of the Bahá'ís of Papua and New Guinea with its seat in Lae, and ten during Riḍván 1970: six in Africa, the National Spiritual Assemblies of the Bahá'ís of the Congo Republic (Kinshasa); Ghana; Dahomey, Togo and Niger; Malawi; Botswana; and Gambia, Sénégal, Portuguese Guinea and the Cape Verde Islands; one in the Americas, the National Spiritual Assembly of the Bahá'ís of the Guianas; one in Asia, the National Spiritual Assembly of the Bahá'ís of the Near East; and two in Australasia, the National Spiritual Assemblies of the Bahá'ís of Tonga and the Cook Islands; and Samoa. Thus at Riḍván 1970 the number of National Spiritual Assemblies will be raised to ninety-three.

In harmony with the worldwide growth of the Cause the World Center of the Faith is also developing rapidly. The pilgrims, the beloved Guardian has said, are the lifeblood of this World Center and it has long been our cherished hope and desire to be able to grant the bounty of pilgrimage to the Holy Land to all who can avail themselves of it. It is therefore with great joy that we now find it possible to open the door of pilgrimage to a much greater number of believers. Beginning in October of this year the size of each group of friends to be invited will be quadrupled and the number of groups each year will be increased so that nearly six times the present number of pilgrims will have the opportunity each year to pray in the Shrines of the Central Figures of their Faith, to visit the places hallowed by the footsteps, sufferings and triumphs of Bahá'u'lláh and 'Abdu'l-Bahá, and to meditate in the tranquillity of these sacred precincts, beautified with so much loving care by our beloved Guardian.

This increased flow of pilgrims will greatly augment the spiritual development of the Bahá'í World Community which now, after five years of strenuous labor and bearing the laurels of outstanding victories, is entering the fourth phase of the Nine Year Plan.

The great, the most pressing need, at this stage of the Plan, is a rapid increase in the number of believers, and a major advance in the opening of the additional localities as well as in the formation of the well grounded Local Spiritual Assemblies called for in the Plan. This worldwide activity, the hallmark of the fourth phase of the Plan, answering the tremendous opportunities offered by the present condition of mankind, will be strongly reinforced by the continuance of proclamation, is the essential foundation for the erection of the remaining National Spiritual Assemblies, and will increasingly witness to the benefits of international traveling teaching and inter-Assembly cooperation. Above all, it requires a sacrificial outpouring by the friends of contributions in support of the Funds of the Faith, and the raising up of a mighty host of pioneers.

During the second year of the Plan the Bahá'í world achieved its greatest feat of organized pioneering when a total of five hundred and five believers arose to settle in the unopened and weakly held territories of the earth. This magnificent achievement must now be surpassed. The call is raised for seven hundred and thirty-three believers to leave their homes and settle in territories of the globe in dire need of pioneer support or as yet unopened to the Faith. These devoted believers, who should arise without delay, are needed to settle, during the fourth phase of the Plan, in 184 specified territories of the globe: 48 in Africa, 40 in the Americas, 40 in Asia, 18 in Australasia and 38 in Europe. Although primary responsibility has been assigned to those national Bahá'í communities most able to provide pioneers, all should ponder in their hearts whether they too cannot respond to this call, either by going themselves or by deputizing, in response to Bahá'u'lláh's injunction, those who can go in their stead. Detailed information is being sent to National Spiritual Assemblies to ensure that this vital mobilization of Bahá'í warriors is accomplished as quickly as possible.

Beloved Friends, the Nine Year Plan is well advanced, our work is blessed by the never-ceasing confirmations of Bahá'u'lláh, and the entire Bahá'í World Community is committed to complete victory. That happy consummation, now faintly discernible on the far horizon, will be reached through hard work, realistic planning, sacrificial deeds, intensification of the teaching work and, above all, through constant endeavor on the part of every single Bahá'í to conform his inner life to that glorious ideal set for mankind by Bahá'u'lláh and exemplified by 'Abdu'l-Bahá. In contemplating the Master's divine example we may well reflect that His life and deeds were not acted to a pattern of expediency, but were the inevitable and spontaneous expression of His inner self. We, likewise, shall act according to His example only as our inward spirits, growing and maturing through the disciplines of prayer and practice of the Teachings, become the wellsprings of all our attitudes and actions. This will promote the accomplishment of God's purpose; this will ensure the triumph of His Faith and enable us to build up the present motion of the Cause into a grand momentum whose force will carry the community of the Most Great Name to glorious victory in 1973 and onwards to the as yet unapprehended vistas of the Most Great Peace.

THE UNIVERSAL HOUSE OF JUSTICE

Guidance on Self-Defense

26 May 1969

National Spiritual Assembly of the
 Bahá'ís of Canada

Dear Bahá'í Friends,

We have reviewed your letter of April 11th, asking about the teachings of the Faith on self-defense and any guidance on individual conduct in the face of increasing civil disorder in North American cities.

From the texts you already have available it is clear that Bahá'u'lláh has stated that is preferable to be killed in the path of God's good-pleasure than to kill, and that organized religious attack against Bahá'ís should never turn into any kind of warfare, as this is strictly prohibited in our Writings.

A hitherto untranslated Tablet from 'Abdu'l-Bahá, however, points out that in the case of attack by robbers and highwaymen, a Bahá'í should not surrender himself, but should try, as far as circumstances permit, to defend himself, and later on lodge a complaint with the government authorities. In a letter written on behalf of the Guardian, he also indicates that in an emergency when there is no legal force at hand to appeal to, a Bahá'í is justified in defending his life. In another letter the Guardian has further pointed out that the assault of an irresponsible assailant upon a Bahá'í should be resisted by the Bahá'í, who would be justified, under such circumstances, in protecting his life.

The House of Justice does not wish at the present time to go beyond the guidelines given in the above-mentioned statements. The question is basically a matter of conscience, and in each case the Bahá'í involved must use his judgment in determining when to stop in self-defense lest his action deteriorate into retaliation.

Of course the above principles apply also in cases when a Bahá'í finds himself involved in situations of civil disorder. We have, however, advised the National Spiritual Assembly of the United States that under the present circumstances in that country it is preferable that Bahá'ís do not buy nor own arms for their protection or the protection of their families.

With loving Bahá'í greetings,
THE UNIVERSAL HOUSE OF JUSTICE

Homefront Victories in the United States

25 June 1969

National Spiritual Assembly of the
  Bahá'ís of the United States.

Dear Bahá'í Friends,

The news of the homefront victories contained in your Riḍván cable and in your semiannual statistical report brought great joy to our hearts. The members of your valiant community have clearly demonstrated their staunch resolve and their understanding of their task to strengthen the homefront as they simultaneously pursue their global mission. They have poured their funds freely and generously into the international teaching work of the Faith through substantial contributions to the Bahá'í Fund, have assisted their sister communities around the world with the purchase of sorely needed national properties and, as the pioneers have arisen and gone forth in troops to ensure the spiritual conquest of the planet, new believers have embraced the Cause on the homefront, resulting in more than 300 new localities being opened to the Faith and the formation of 45 additional Local Spiritual Assemblies at Riḍván, thus establishing an enlarged base of operations from which additional pioneers must now go forth to further illumine and strengthen the five continents of the globe.

You may be assured that we shall continue to remember you in our prayers at the Holy Shrines, supplicating that Bahá'u'lláh will guide, bless and sustain you, individually and collectively, as you continue to labor to execute your numerous and varied responsibilities.

With loving Bahá'í greetings
THE UNIVERSAL HOUSE OF JUSTICE

Appointments to Continental Boards of Counselors

10 July 1969

To: National Spiritual Assemblies

Dear Bahá'í Friends,

With great joy we announce that we have decided to increase the total number of members of the Continental Boards of Counselors for the Protection and Propagation of the Faith to thirty-eight by adding John McHenry III to the Continental Board of Counselors in North East Asia and Mas'úd Khamsí to the Continental Board of Counselors in South America, raising the number of Counselors on each Board to three and four, respectively.

We also rejoice to announce the appointment of Mrs. Shirin Boman to the Continental Board of Counselors of Western Asia to fill a vacancy on that Board.

The devoted efforts of all eleven Continental Boards of Counselors during the first year of their service to the Faith of Bahá'u'lláh have been most exemplary and praiseworthy. We are deeply grateful for the loyalty, steadfastness and devotion which have characterized the activities of all members in reinforcing the vitally important work of the Hands of the Cause of God.

Please share these glad tidings with the friends.

With loving Bahá'í greetings,
THE UNIVERSAL HOUSE OF JUSTICE

Formation of an Additional National Spiritual Assembly during Riḍván 1970

11 August 1969

To: All National Spiritual Assemblies

Dear Bahá'í Friends,

In the brief space of time following the announcement of the formation of six new National Spiritual Assemblies in

Africa next Riḍván, the succession of victories, resulting from the prodigious efforts exerted by the devoted friends, impels us to announce that a seventh National Spiritual Assembly will be formed in Africa at Riḍván, 1970. The new National Spiritual Assembly including Congo (Brazzaville), Chad, Central African Republic and Gabon, will have its seat in Bangui. This will leave Uganda with its own separate National Spiritual Assembly.

Please share this joyous news with the believers. We know the friends throughout the world join us in our supplications for the continued, uninterrupted prosecution and speedy fulfillment of the goals, terminating in the ultimate triumph of the Cause of Bahá'u'lláh.

> With loving Bahá'í greetings,
> THE UNIVERSAL HOUSE OF JUSTICE

Work of Continental Boards of Counselors and Auxiliary Board Members

1 October 1969

To: The Continental Boards of Counselors and
National Spiritual Assemblies.

Dear Bahá'í Friends,

A number of questions have been raised concerning the work of the Counselors and Auxiliary Board members, and it has been suggested that Auxiliary Board members be permitted to work regularly with National Spiritual Assemblies and national committees. We have carefully considered again the various factors involved and have decided that we must uphold the principle that such direct consultations should be exceptional rather than the rule.

It is the responsibility of Spiritual Assemblies, assisted by their committees, to organize and direct the teaching work, and in doing so they must, naturally, also do all they can to stimulate and inspire the friends. It is, however, inevitable that the Assemblies and committees, being burdened with the administration of the teaching work as well as with all other aspects of Bahá'í community life, will be unable to spend as much time as they would wish on stimulating the believers.

Authority and direction flow from the Assemblies, whereas the power to accomplish the tasks resides primarily in the entire body of the believers. It is the principal task of the Auxiliary Boards to assist in arousing and releasing this power. This is a vital activity, and if they are to be able to perform it adequately they must avoid becoming involved in the work of administration. For example, when Auxiliary Board members arouse believers to pioneer, any believer who expresses his desire to do so should be referred to the appropriate committee which will then organize the project. Counselors and Auxiliary Board members should not, themselves, organize pioneering or travel teaching projects. Thus it is seen that the Auxiliary Boards should work closely with the grass roots of the community: the individual believers, groups and Local Spiritual Assemblies, advising, stimulating and assisting them. The Counselors are responsible for stimulating, counseling and assisting National Spiritual Assemblies, and also work with individuals, groups and Local Assemblies.

It is always possible, of course, for Counselors to depute an Auxiliary Board member to meet with a National Spiritual Assembly for a particular purpose, but this should not become a regular practice. Similarly, if the National Spiritual Assembly agrees, it may be advisable for an Auxiliary Board member to meet occasionally with a national committee to clarify the situation in the area and share information and ideas thoroughly. But this also should not become regular. Were it to do so there would be grave danger of inhibiting the proper working of these two institutions, vitiating and undermining the collaboration that must essentially exist between the Continental Boards of Counselors and National Spiritual Assemblies. It would diffuse the energies and time of the Auxiliary Board members through their becoming involved in the administration of teaching. It could lead to the Auxiliary Board member's gradually taking over the direction of the national committee, usurping the function of the National Assembly, or to his becoming merely a traveling teacher sent hither and thither at the direction of the committee or National Assembly.

It is, of course, vital that information be shared fully and promptly, as has been explained in the compilation on the work of Auxiliary Board members that was circulated on March 25, 1969. The ways of ensuring this should be worked out by the Counselors and National Spiritual Assemblies and methods may vary from area to area.

Reports and recommendations for action, however, are quite different. Auxiliary Board members should send theirs to the Counselors and not to National Assemblies or national committees directly. It is possible that the Counselors may reject or modify the recommendation; or, if they accept it and pass it on to the National Spiritual Assembly, the National Assembly may decide to refuse it. For an Auxiliary Board member to make recommendations directly to a national committee would lose the benefit of knowledge and experience in a wider field than that of which the Auxiliary Board member is aware, and would short-circuit and undermine the authority of both the Counselors and the National Assembly.

Similarly, although an Auxiliary Board member can and should receive information from the National Assemblies and national committees, his primary source of information about the community should be his own direct contacts with Local Spiritual Assemblies, groups and individual believers. In this way the Counselors as well as the National Spiritual Assemblies have the benefit of two independent sources of information about the community: through the Auxiliary Board members on the one hand, and through the national committees on the other.

Assemblies sometimes misunderstand what is meant by the statement that Counselors and Auxiliary Board members are concerned with the teaching work and not with administration. It is taken to mean that they may not give advice on administrative matters. This is quite wrong. One of the things that Counselors and Auxiliary Board members should watch and report on is the proper working of administrative institutions. The statement that they do not have anything to do with administration means, simply, that they do not administer. They do not direct or organize the teaching work nor do they adjudicate in matters of personal conflict or personal problems. All these activities fall within the sphere of responsibility of the Spiritual Assemblies. But if an Auxiliary Board member finds a Local Spiritual Assembly functioning incorrectly he should call its attention to the appropriate Texts; likewise if, in his work with the community, an Auxiliary Board member finds that the teaching work is being held up by inefficiency of national committees, he should report this in detail to the Counselors who will then decide whether to refer it to the National Spiritual Assembly concerned. Similarly, if the Counselors find that a National Spiritual Assembly is not functioning properly, they should not hesitate to consult with the National Spiritual Assembly about this in a frank and loving way.

It is the Spiritual Assemblies who plan and direct the work, but these plans should be well known to the Counselors and Auxiliary Board members, because one of the ways in which they can assist the Assemblies is by urging the believers continually to support the plans of the Assemblies. If a National Spiritual Assembly has adopted one goal as preeminent in a year, the Auxiliary Board members should bear this in mind in all their contacts with the believers and should direct their attention to the plans of the National Assembly, and stimulate them to enthusiastically support them.

The Counselors in each continental zone have wide latitude in the carrying out of their work. Likewise they should give to each Auxiliary Board member considerable freedom of action within his own allocated area. Although the Counselors should regularly direct the work of the Auxiliary Board members, the latter should realize that they need not wait for direction; the nature of their work is such that they should be continually engaged in it according to their own best judgment, even if they are given no specific tasks to perform. Above all the Auxiliary Board members should build up a warm and loving relationship between themselves and the believers in their area so that the Local Spiritual Assemblies will spontaneously turn to them for advice and assistance.

We assure you all of our fervent prayers in the Holy Shrines for the blessings of Bahá'u'lláh upon the strenuous and highly meritorious services that you are performing with such devotion in His path.

THE UNIVERSAL HOUSE OF JUSTICE

Appeal to Increase Teaching Efforts amidst Catastrophic Events of the Day

16 November 1969

To the Bahá'ís of the World

Dear Friends,

In the worsening world situation, fraught with pain of war, violence and the sudden uprooting of long-established institutions, can be seen the fulfillment of the prophecies of Bahá'u'lláh and the oft-repeated warnings of the Master and the beloved Guardian about the inevitable fate of a lamentably defective social system, an unenlightened leadership and a rebellious and unbelieving humanity. Governments and peoples of both the developed and developing nations, and other human institutions, secular and religious, finding themselves helpless to reverse the trend of the catastrophic events of the day, stand bewildered and overpowered by the magnitude and complexity of the problems facing them. At this fateful hour in human history many, unfortunately, seem content to stand aside and wring their hands in despair or else join in the babel of shouting and protestation which loudly objects, but offers no solution to the woes and afflictions plaguing our age.

Nevertheless a greater and greater number of thoughtful and fair-minded men and women are recognizing in the clamor of contention, grief and destruction, now reaching such horrendous proportions, the evidences of Divine chastisement, and turning their faces towards God are becoming increasingly receptive to His Word. Doubtless the present circumstances, though tragic and awful in their immediate consequences, are serving to sharpen the focus on the indispensability of the Teachings of Bahá'u'lláh to the needs of the present age, and will provide many opportunities to reach countless waiting souls, hungry and thirsty for Divine guidance.

It is these opportunities which we must seize before it is too late. What is needed now is the awakening of all believers to the immediacy of the challenge so that each may assume his share of the responsibility for taking the Teachings to all humanity. Universal participation, a salient objective of the Nine Year Plan, must be pressed toward attainment in every continent, country and island of the globe. Every Bahá'í, however humble or inarticulate, must become intent on fulfilling his role as a bearer of the Divine Message. Indeed, how can a true believer remain silent while around us men cry out in anguish for truth, love and unity to descend upon this world?

We all know how often the Master and the beloved Guardian called upon the friends to consciously strive to be more loving, more united, more dedicated and prayerful than ever before in order to overcome the atmosphere of present-day society which is unloving, disunited, careless of right and wrong and heedless of God. "When we see the increasing darkness in the world today," the Guardian's secretary wrote on his behalf, "we can fully realize that unless the Message of Bahá'u'lláh reaches into the hearts of men and transforms them, there can be no peace and no spiritual progress in the future."

The Nine Year Plan is the current stage in the achievement of that sublime objective. It is now imperative for every Bahá'í to set for himself individual teaching goals. The admonition of 'Abdu'l-Bahá to lead at least one new soul to the Faith each year and the exhortation of Shoghi Effendi to hold a Bahá'í fireside in one's home every Bahá'í month are examples of individual goals. Many have capacities to do even more, but this alone will assure final and complete victory for the Plan.

We call upon the friends to join with us in prayer during the Feast of Sulṭán that we will all become so imbued with zeal, courage and enthusiasm that from this day to the end of the Nine Year Plan nothing will be able to stay the victorious onward march of the followers of the Most Great Name. May our efforts be worthy of the blessings and confirmations of Bahá'u'lláh.

With loving Bahá'í greetings,
THE UNIVERSAL HOUSE OF JUSTICE

Acquisition of Property Adjacent to Bahjí

18 November 1969

To: National Spiritual Assemblies

Dear Bahá'í Friends,

Enclosed please find our letter of 16 November 1969 addressed to the Bahá'ís of the World.* Please share this letter

*See pp. 33-35.

with all believers in your jurisdiction as soon as possible.

After several years of protracted negotiations with agencies of the Israel Government both in Jerusalem and Haifa, an important property adjacent to Bahjí and embracing the Master's tea house has been acquired. On November 17th we cabled the National Spiritual Assembly of the United States as follows:

> With grateful hearts announce successful conclusion formal negotiations initiated nearly two decades ago by beloved Guardian with authorities State Israel resulting ownership vitally needed property surrounding 'Abdu'l-Bahá's teahouse immediate neighborhood Most Holy Tomb Founder Faith. Acquisition much desired land extending gardens Bahjí facilitated through exchange property dedicated some thirtysix years ago to Holy Tomb Bahá'u'lláh by devoted servant Cause Ḥájí 'Alí Yazdí (Signed) Universal House of Justice.

The successful conclusion of these negotiations initiated during the lifetime of the beloved Guardian was made possible through the acceptance by the Government, as even exchange, of an endowment property given to the Faith in 1933 by the late Ḥájí 'Alí Yazdí. The significance of the specific piece of land donated by this venerable soul becomes apparent when reading the following quotation from the IN MEMORIAM article about him in *The Bahá'í World*, Volume IX:

> He will forever be remembered, amongst other things, as the establisher of Bahá'í endowments in the vicinity of 'Akká through his gift of a tract of land dedicated to Bahá'u'lláh's Holy Tomb in Bahjí . . .

It is a glowing tribute to the memory of this devoted servant of the Blessed Beauty that his gift should play such an important part in securing this valuable additional safeguard for the Most Holy Tomb.

Please also convey the news of this victory to the friends.

With loving Bahá'í greetings,
THE UNIVERSAL HOUSE OF JUSTICE

Comments on the Guardianship and The Universal House of Justice

7 December 1969

Dear Bahá'í Friend,*

Your recent letter, in which you share with us the questions that have occurred to some of the youth in studying "The Dispensation of Bahá'u'lláh," has been carefully considered, and we feel that we should comment both on the particular passage you mention and on a related passage in the same work, because both bear on the relationship between the Guardianship and the Universal House of Justice.

The first passage concerns the Guardian's duty to insist upon a reconsideration by his fellow-members in the Universal House of Justice of any enactment which he believes conflicts with the meaning and departs from the spirit of the Sacred Writings. The second passage concerns the infallibility of the Universal House of Justice without the Guardian, namely Shoghi Effendi's statement that "Without such an institution [the Guardianship] . . . the necessary guidance to define the sphere of the legislative action of its elected representatives would be totally withdrawn."

Some of the youth, you indicate, were puzzled as to how to reconcile the former of these two passages with such state-

---

* A letter addressed to a new believer.

ments as that in the Will of 'Abdu'l-Bahá which affirms that the Universal House of Justice is "freed from all error."

Just as the Will and Testament of 'Abdu'l-Bahá does not in any way contradict the Kitáb-i-Aqdas but, in the Guardian's words, "confirms, supplements, and correlates the provisions of the Aqdas," so the writings of the Guardian contradict neither the revealed Word nor the interpretations of the Master. In attempting to understand the Writings, therefore, one must first realize that there is and can be no real contradiction in them, and in the light of this we can confidently seek the unity of meaning which they contain.

The Guardian and the Universal House of Justice have certain duties and functions in common; each also operates within a separate and distinct sphere. As Shoghi Effendi explained, ". . . it is made indubitably clear and evident that the Guardian of the Faith has been made the Interpreter of the Word and that the Universal House of Justice has been invested with the function of legislating on matters not expressly revealed in the teachings. The interpretation of the Guardian, functioning within his own sphere, is as authoritative and binding as the enactments of the International House of Justice, whose exclusive right and prerogative is to pronounce upon and deliver the final judgment on such laws and ordinances as Bahá'u'lláh has not expressly revealed." He goes on to affirm, "Neither can, nor will ever, infringe upon the sacred and prescribed domain of the other. Neither will seek to curtail the specific and undoubted authority with which both have been divinely invested." It is impossible to conceive that two centers of authority, which the Master has stated "are both under the care and protection of the Abhá Beauty, under the shelter and unerring guidance of His Holiness the Exalted One," could conflict with one another, because both are vehicles of the same Divine Guidance.

The Universal House of Justice, beyond its function as the enactor of legislation, has been invested with the more general functions of protecting and administering the Cause, solving obscure questions and deciding upon matters that have caused difference. Nowhere is it stated that the infallibility of the Universal House of Justice is by virtue of the Guardian's membership or presence on that body. Indeed, 'Abdu'l-Bahá in His Will and Shoghi Effendi in his "Dispensation of Bahá'u'lláh" have both explicitly stated that the elected members of the Universal House of Justice in consultation are recipients of unfailing Divine Guidance. Furthermore the Guardian himself in "The World Order of Bahá'u'lláh" asserted that "It must be also clearly understood by every believer that the institution of Guardianship does not under any circumstances abrogate, or even in the slightest degree detract from, the powers granted to the Universal House of Justice by Bahá'u'lláh in the Kitáb-i-Aqdas, and repeatedly and solemnly confirmed by 'Abdu'l-Bahá in His Will. It does not constitute in any manner a contradiction to the Will and Writings of Bahá'u'lláh, nor does it nullify any of His revealed instructions."

While the specific responsibility of the Guardian is the interpretation of the Word, he is also invested with all the powers and prerogatives necessary to discharge his function as Guardian of the Cause, its Head and supreme protector. He is, furthermore, made the irremovable head and member for life of the supreme legislative body of the Faith. It is as the head of the Universal House of Justice, and as a member of that body, that the Guardian takes part in the process of legislation. If the following passage, which gave rise to your query, is considered as referring to this last relationship, you will see that there is no contradiction between it and the other texts: "Though the Guardian of the Faith has been made the permanent head of so august a body he can never, even temporarily, assume the right of exclusive legislation. He cannot override the decision of the majority of his fellow-members, but is bound to insist upon a reconsideration by them of any enactment he conscientiously believes to conflict with the meaning and to depart from the spirit of Bahá'u'lláh's revealed utterances."

Although the Guardian, in relation to his fellow-members within the Universal House of Justice, cannot override the decision of the majority, it is inconceivable that the other members would ignore any objection he raised in the course of consultation or pass legislation contrary to what he expressed as being in harmony with the spirit of the Cause. It is, after all, the final act of judgment delivered by the Universal House of Justice that is vouchsafed infallibility, not any views expressed in the course of the process of enactment.

It can be seen, therefore, that there is no conflict between the Master's statements concerning the unfailing divine guidance conferred upon the Universal House of Justice and the above passage from "The Dispensation of Bahá'u'lláh."

It may help the friends to understand this relationship if they are aware of some of the processes that the Universal House of Justice follows when legislating. First, of course, it observes the greatest care in studying the Sacred Texts and the interpretations of the Guardian as well as considering the views of all the members. After long consultation the process of drafting a pronouncement is put into effect. During this process the whole matter may well be reconsidered. As a result of such reconsideration the final judgment may be significantly different from the conclusion earlier favored, or possibly it may be decided not to legislate at all on that subject at that time. One can understand how great would be the attention paid to the views of the Guardian during the above process were he alive.

In considering the second passage we must once more hold fast to the principle that the teachings do not contradict themselves.

Future Guardians are clearly envisaged and referred to in the Writings, but there is nowhere any promise or guarantee

that the line of Guardians would endure forever; on the
contrary there are clear indications that the line could be
broken. Yet, in spite of this, there is a repeated insistence in
the Writings on the indestructibility of the Covenant and the
immutability of God's Purpose for this Day.

One of the most striking passages which envisage the possi-
bility of such a break in the line of Guardians is in the
Kitáb-i-Aqdas itself:

> The endowments dedicated to charity revert to God, the
> Revealer of Signs. No one has the right to lay hold on them
> without leave from the Dawning-Place of Revelation. After
> Him the decision rests with the Aghsán (Branches), and
> after them with the House of Justice—should it be estab-
> lished in the world by then—so that they may use these
> endowments for the benefit of the Sites exalted in this
> Cause, and for that which they have been commanded by
> God, the Almighty, the All-Powerful. Otherwise the en-
> dowments should be referred to the people of Bahá, who
> speak not without His leave and who pass no judgment but
> in accordance with that which God has ordained in this
> Tablet, they who are the champions of victory betwixt
> heaven and earth, so that they may spend them on that
> which has been decreed in the Holy Book by God, the
> Mighty, the Bountiful.

The passing of Shoghi Effendi in 1957 precipitated the very
situation provided for in this passage, in that the line of Aghsán
ended before the House of Justice had been elected. Although, as is seen, the ending of the line of Aghsán at some
stage was provided for, we must never underestimate the
grievous loss that the Faith has suffered. God's purpose for
mankind remains unchanged, however, and the mighty Covenant of Bahá'u'lláh remains impregnable. Has not
Bahá'u'lláh stated categorically, "The Hand of Omnipotence
hath established His Revelation upon an unassailable, an

enduring foundation." While 'Abdu'l-Bahá confirms: "Verily, God effecteth that which He pleaseth; naught can annul His Covenant; naught can obstruct His favor nor oppose His Cause!" "Everything is subject to corruption; but the Covenant of thy Lord shall continue to pervade all regions." "The tests of every dispensation are in direct proportion to the greatness of the Cause and as heretofore such a manifest Covenant, written by the Supreme Pen, has not been entered upon, the tests are proportionately severe . . . These agitations of the violators are no more than the foam of the ocean, . . . this froth of the ocean shall not endure and shall soon disappear and vanish, while on the other hand the ocean of the Covenant shall eternally surge and roar." And Shoghi Effendi has clearly stated: "The bedrock on which this Administrative Order is founded is God's immutable Purpose for mankind in this day." ". . . this priceless gem of Divine Revelation, now still in its embryonic state, shall evolve within the shell of His Law, and shall forge ahead, undivided and unimpaired, till it embraces the whole of mankind."

In the Bahá'í Faith there are two authoritative centers appointed to which the believers must turn, for in reality the Interpreter of the Word is an extension of that center which is the Word itself. The Book is the record of the utterance of Bahá'u'lláh, while the divinely inspired Interpreter is the living Mouth of that Book—it is he and he alone who can authoritatively state what the Book means. Thus one center is the Book with its Interpreter, and the other is the Universal House of Justice guided by God to decide on whatever is not explicitly revealed in the Book. This pattern of centers and their relationships is apparent at every stage in the unfoldment of the Cause. In the Kitáb-i-Aqdas Bahá'u'lláh tells the believers to refer after His passing to the Book, and to "Him Whom God hath purposed, Who hath branched from this Ancient Root." In the Kitáb-i-'Ahdí (the Book of Bahá'u'lláh's Covenant), He makes it clear that this reference is to 'Abdu'l-Bahá.

In the Aqdas Bahá'u'lláh also ordains the institution of the Universal House of Justice, and confers upon it the powers necessary for it to discharge its ordained functions. The Master in His Will and Testament explicitly institutes the Guardianship, which Shoghi Effendi states was clearly anticipated in the verses of the Kitáb-i-Aqdas, reaffirms and elucidates the authority of the Universal House of Justice, and refers the believers once again to the Book: "Unto the Most Holy Book everyone must turn and all that is not expressly recorded therein must be referred to the Universal House of Justice," and at the very end of the Will He says: "All must seek guidance and turn unto the Center of the Cause and the House of Justice. And he that turneth unto whatsoever else is indeed in grievous error."

As the sphere of jurisdiction of the Universal House of Justice in matters of legislation extends to whatever is not explicitly revealed in the Sacred Text, it is clear that the Book itself is the highest authority and delimits the sphere of action of the House of Justice. Likewise, the Interpreter of the Book must also have the authority to define the sphere of the legislative action of the elected representatives of the Cause. The writings of the Guardian and the advice given by him over the thirty-six years of his Guardianship show the way in which he exercised this function in relation to the Universal House of Justice as well as to National and Local Spiritual Assemblies.

The fact that the Guardian has the authority to define the sphere of the legislative action of the Universal House of Justice does not carry with it the corollary that without such guidance the Universal House of Justice might stray beyond the limits of its proper authority; such a deduction would conflict with all the other texts referring to its infallibility, and specifically with the Guardian's own clear assertion that the Universal House of Justice never can or will infringe on the sacred and prescribed domain of the Guardianship. It should be remembered, however, that although National and Local

Spiritual Assemblies can receive divine guidance if they consult in the manner and spirit described by 'Abdu'l-Bahá, they do not share in the explicit guarantees of infallibility conferred upon the Universal House of Justice. Any careful student of the Cause can see with what care the Guardian, after the passing of 'Abdu'l-Bahá, guided these elected representatives of the believers in the painstaking erection of the Administrative Order and in the formulation of Local and National Bahá'í Constitutions.

We hope that these elucidations will assist the friends in understanding these relationships more clearly, but we must all remember that we stand too close to the beginnings of the System ordained by Bahá'u'lláh to be able fully to understand its potentialities or the interrelationships of its component parts. As Shoghi Effendi's secretary wrote on his behalf to an individual believer on 25 March 1930, "The contents of the Will of the Master are far too much for the present generation to comprehend. It needs at least a century of actual working before the treasures of wisdom hidden in it can be revealed . . ."

With loving Bahá'í greetings,
THE UNIVERSAL HOUSE OF JUSTICE

Noninterference in Political Affairs

8 February 1970

To: National Spiritual Assemblies in Africa

Dear Bahá'í Friends,

For long centuries the African Continent, or rather that great part of it which lies south of the Sahara, remained relatively isolated from the rest of the world, untroubled and scarcely touched by the surging conflicts of the nations to the north and east. Now, rapidly emerging into the main stream of international interest, the African peoples, who were compared by Bahá'u'lláh to the black pupil of the eye through which "the light of the spirit shineth forth," are being swept by the heady enthusiasms of new-found independence, torn by the conflicting forces of divergent political interests, their vision obscured by the haze of materialism and the dust of nationalistic passions and age-old tribal rivalries.

In the midst of the storm and stress of the battles of selfish interests being waged about them, stand the followers of the Most Great Name, their sight attracted to the rising Sun of God's Holy Cause, their hearts welded together in a bond of true unity with all the children of men, and their voices raised in a universal song of praise to the Glory of God and the oneness of mankind, calling on their fellowmen to forget and forgo their differences and join them in obedience and service to God's Holy Command in this Day.

The Army of the Cause, advancing at the bidding of the Lord, to conquer the hearts of men, can never be defeated, but its rate of advance can be slowed down by acts of unwisdom and ignorance on the part of its supporters. We are writing you this letter to help in clarifying some of the issues that have, in the past, blurred the vision of some of the believers, and caused them to commit errors of judgment which have retarded the progress of the Faith in their countries.

One of these issues, and by far the most important, is a lack of appreciation of the implications of the Bahá'í principle of noninterference in political affairs. We find that 'Abdu'l-Bahá and Shoghi Effendi have given us clear and convincing reasons why we must uphold this principle. These reasons are summarized below for the study and deepening of the friends. It is our hope that these observations will not only help the friends to intelligently and radiantly follow the holy teachings on this matter, but will help them to explain the Bahá'í attitude to those who may question its wisdom and usefulness:

The Faith of God is the sole source of salvation for mankind today. The true cause of the ills of humanity is its disunity. No matter how perfect may be the machinery devised by the leaders of men for the political unity of the world, it will still not provide the antidote to the poison sapping the vigor of present-day society. These ills can be cured only through the instrumentality of God's Faith. There are many well-wishers of mankind who devote their efforts to relief-work and charity and to the material well-being of man, but only Bahá'ís can do the work which God most wants done. When we devote ourselves to the work of the Faith we are doing a work which is the greatest aid and only refuge for a needy and divided world.

The Bahá'í Community is a worldwide organization seeking to establish true and universal peace on earth. If a Bahá'í works for one political party to overcome another it is a negation of the very spirit of the Faith. Membership in any political party, therefore, necessarily entails repudiation of some or all of the principles of peace and unity proclaimed by Bahá'u'lláh. As 'Abdu'l-Bahá stated: "Our party is God's party; we do not belong to any party."

If a Bahá'í were to insist on his right to support a certain political party he could not deny the same degree of freedom to other believers. This would mean that within the ranks of the Faith, whose primary mission is to unite all men as one great family under God, there would be Bahá'ís opposed to each other. Where, then, would be the example of unity and harmony which the world is seeking?

If the institutions of the Faith, God forbid, became involved in politics, the Bahá'ís would find themselves arousing antagonism instead of love. If they took one stand in one country, they would be bound to change the views of the people in another country about the aims and purposes of the Faith. By becoming involved in political disputes, the Bahá'ís instead of changing the world or helping it, would themselves be lost and destroyed. The world situation is so confused and moral issues which were once clear have become so mixed up with selfish and battling factions, that the best way Bahá'ís can serve the highest interests of their country and the cause of true salvation for the world, is to sacrifice their political pursuits and affiliations and wholeheartedly and fully support the divine system of Bahá'u'lláh.

The Faith is not opposed to the true interests of any nation, nor is it against any party or faction. It holds aloof from all controversies and transcends them all, while enjoining upon its followers loyalty to government and a sane patriotism. This love for their country the Bahá'ís show by serving its well-being in their daily activity, or by working in the administrative channels of the government instead of through party politics or in diplomatic or political posts. The Bahá'ís may, indeed are encouraged to, mix with all strata of society, with the highest authorities and with leading personalities as well as with the mass of the people, and should bring the knowledge of the Faith to them; but in so doing they should strictly avoid becoming identified, or identifying the Faith, with political pursuits and party programs.

So vital is this principle of noninterference in political matters, which must govern the acts and words of Bahá'ís in every land, that Shoghi Effendi has written that "Neither the charges which the uninformed and the malicious may be led to bring against them, nor the allurements of honors and rewards" would ever induce the true believers to deviate from this path, and that their words and conduct must proclaim that the followers of Bahá'u'lláh "are actuated by no selfish ambition, that they neither thirst for power, nor mind any wave of unpopularity, of distrust or criticism, which a strict adherence to their standards might provoke."

"Difficult and delicate though be our task," he continues, "the sustaining power of Bahá'u'lláh and of His Divine guidance will assuredly assist us, if we follow steadfastly in His way, and strive to uphold the integrity of His laws. The light of His redeeming grace, which no earthly power can obscure, will if we persevere, illuminate our path, as we steer our course amid the snares and pitfalls of a troubled age and will enable us to discharge our duties in a manner that would redound to the glory and honor of His blessed Name."

The second issue which causes difficulties for the African friends in these days is the matter of tribalism. As Bahá'ís they are convinced that mankind is one and must be viewed as one entity, yet, as members of their respective tribes, they find themselves expected by their non-Bahá'í brothers to give their first loyalty to, and even aggressively pursue the interests of their tribe. They live, moreover, in an atmosphere which is only too often one of mistrust, fear and even hatred against the members of other tribes.

The Bahá'í attitude in such a situation is clearly set forth in the Writings. As Bahá'ís we are attached to our tribes and clans, just as we are to our families and, on a larger scale, to our nations, but we do not allow this attachment to conflict with our wider loyalty to humanity. The followers of the Faith, the Guardian has clearly stated, "will not hesitate to subordinate every particular interest, be it personal, regional or national, to the overriding interests of the generality of mankind, knowing full well that in a world of interdependent peoples and nations the advantage of the part is best to be reached by the advantage of the whole, and that no lasting result can be achieved by any of the component parts if the general interests of the entity itself are neglected."

In further elucidating this theme he has written: "Let there be no misgivings as to the animating purpose of the worldwide Law of Bahá'u'lláh . . . It does not ignore, nor does it attempt to suppress, the diversity of ethnical origins, of climate, of history, of language and tradition, of thought and habit, that differentiate the peoples and nations of the world. It calls for a wider loyalty, for a larger aspiration than any that has animated the human race. It insists upon the subordination of national impulses and interests to the imperative claims of a unified world. It repudiates excessive centralization on one hand, and disclaims all attempts at uniformity on the other. Its watchword is unity in diversity . . ."

In these days when tribal tensions are increasing in Africa the friends should be vigilant lest any trace of prejudice or hatred, God forbid, may enter their midst. On the contrary, they should endeavor to bring into the Faith an ever larger representation of the various tribes in each country, and through complete lack of prejudice as well as through the love that Bahá'ís have for each other and for their non-Bahá'í neighbors, demonstrate to their countrymen what the Word of God can do. They will thus provide, for the scrutiny of the leaders and rulers of their countries, a shining example of a unified community, working together in full concord and harmony, demonstrating a hope that is attainable, and a pattern worthy to be emulated.

To discriminate against any tribes because they are in a minority is a violation of the spirit that animates the Faith of Bahá'u'lláh. As followers of God's Holy Faith it is our obligation to protect the just interests of any minority element within the Bahá'í community. In fact in the administration of our Bahá'í affairs, representatives of minority groups are not only enabled to enjoy equal rights and privileges, but they are even favored and accorded priority. Bahá'ís should be careful never to deviate from this noble standard, even if the course of events or public opinion should bring pressure to bear upon them.

The principles in the Writings are clear, but usually it is when these principles are applied that questions arise. In all cases where the correct course of action is not clear believers should consult their National Spiritual Assembly who will exercise their judgment in advising the friends on the best course to follow.

It is the hope and prayer of the Universal House of Justice that National Spiritual Assemblies in Africa will, in full collaboration with the Continental Boards of Counselors and Auxiliary Boards in their areas, act as loving shepherds to the divine flock in that mighty Continent, protect the friends from the evil influences surrounding them, guide them in the true and right path, and assist them to attain a continuously deeper understanding, a firmer conviction and a more consuming love for the Cause they are so devotedly seeking to promote and serve.

With loving Bahá'í greetings,
THE UNIVERSAL HOUSE OF JUSTICE

Attainment of Consultative Status with the United Nations Economic and Social Council

18 February 1970

To: All National Spiritual Assemblies

Dear Bahá'í Friends,

We share with you the text of a cable sent today to the National Spiritual Assembly of the United States for publication in "Bahá'í News":

Joyfully announce Bahá'í world attainment consultative status United Nations Economic and Social Council thereby fulfilling long cherished hope beloved Guardian and World Center goal Nine Year Plan. Sustained persistent efforts more than twenty years accredited representatives Bahá'í International Community United Nations devoted support Bahá'í communities throughout world finally rewarded. Significant achievement adds prestige influence recognition ever advancing Faith Bahá'u'lláh. Offering prayers gratitude Holy Shrines (Signed) Universal House of Justice.

> With loving Bahá'í greetings,
> THE UNIVERSAL HOUSE OF JUSTICE

The Spirit of Bahá'í Consultation

6 March 1970

National Spiritual Assembly of the
Bahá'ís of Canada.

Dear Bahá'í Friends,

We have your letter of 14 January 1970 asking questions about the decision-making process of Spiritual Assemblies.

It is important to realize that the spirit of Bahá'í consultation is very different from that current in the decision-making processes of non-Bahá'í bodies.

The ideal of Bahá'í consultation is to arrive at a unanimous decision. When this is not possible a vote must be taken. In the words of the beloved Guardian: ". . . when they are called upon to arrive at a certain decision, they should, after dispassionate, anxious and cordial consultation, turn to God in prayer, and with earnestness and conviction and courage record their vote and abide by the voice of the majority, which we are told by the Master to be the voice of truth, never to be challenged, and always to be whole-heartedly enforced."

As soon as a decision is reached it becomes the decision of the whole Assembly, not merely of those members who happened to be among the majority.

When it is proposed to put a matter to the vote, a member of the Assembly may feel that there are additional facts or views which must be sought before he can make up his mind and intelligently vote on the proposition. He should express this feeling to the Assembly, and it is for the Assembly to decide whether or not further consultation is needed before voting.

Whenever it is decided to vote on a proposition all that is required is to ascertain how many of the members are in favor of it; if this is a majority of those present, the motion is carried; if it is a minority, the motion is defeated. Thus the whole question of "abstaining" does not arise in Bahá'í voting. A member who does not vote in favor of a proposition is, in effect, voting against it, even if at that moment he himself feels that he has been unable to make up his mind on the matter.

With loving Bahá'í greetings,
THE UNIVERSAL HOUSE OF JUSTICE

Riḍván Message 1970

Riḍván 1970

To: All National Spiritual Assemblies

Dear Bahá'í Friends,

The following is the text of our message to the Bahá'í world which has been cabled to certain National Spiritual Assemblies:

Bahá'í World Community entering seventh year Nine Year Plan has amply demonstrated ability scale heights devotion sacrifice win astonishing victories world redeeming world healing world uniting Faith. At this Riḍván extend loving welcome eleven new National Spiritual Assemblies now forming seven in Africa one in Americas one in Asia two in Australasia raising to ninetyfour number supporting pillars Universal House Justice. Moved pay loving tribute Hands Cause God their brilliant services blazing teaching trails surface planet uplifting advising Assemblies friends all continents. In view effective reinforcement this noble work by able dedicated Continental Boards Counselors their Auxiliary Boards together with growing need and expansion world community announce augmentation vital institution through appointment three additional Counselors Iraj Ayman western Asia Anneliese Bopp Betty Reed Europe

and authorization appointment fortyfive additional Auxiliary Board members nine Africa sixteen Asia two Australasia eighteen Western Hemisphere. Calling formation
four National Spiritual Assemblies Riḍván 1971 Lesotho
seat Maseru Ivory Coast Mali and Upper Volta seat Abidjan
Trinidad and Tobago seat Port of Spain Solomon Islands
seat Honiara. Nine Year Plan already marked great
achievements pioneering proclamation recognition Faith
upsurge youth acquisition properties commencement construction Panama Temple developments World Center.
Urgent immediate vital need concentrate attention increase
number localities Local Spiritual Assemblies believers fill
remaining pioneer posts. Last Riḍván call raised
sevenhundred and thirtythree pioneers minimum requirement. Fourhundred and seventynine specific posts still
unfilled. Total victory requires more pioneers more funds
more new believers. Hands Cause Counselors Board
Members National Local Spiritual Assemblies every single
follower Bahá'u'lláh summoned utmost effort remaining
years Nine Year Plan. Achievement this step Master's Divine Plan will endow community capacity administrative
agencies undertake next stage implementation supreme
purpose Bahá'u'lláh's revelation unification mankind establishment long promised Kingdom God this earth. Assure
ardent loving prayers Holy Shrines.

With loving Bahá'í greetings,
THE UNIVERSAL HOUSE OF JUSTICE

Second National Youth Conference in the United States

Bahá'í   11 June 1970
Wilmette Illinois USA

Greet representatives vibrant army Bahá'í youth United States
gathered national conference blessed inspiring presence par-

ticipation beloved Amatu'l-Bahá. Growing effectiveness Bahá'í youth evidenced rising tide enrollments and eagerness study exemplify teachings Faith every aspect lives shoulder responsibilities Plan home abroad source joy House Justice and inspiration followers Bahá'u'lláh throughout world. Fervently praying Lord Hosts will bountifully reinforce every effort American Bahá'í youth achieve glorious victories Five Year Plan so audaciously adopted 1968 setting shining example making outstanding contribution completion worldwide Nine Year Plan proclaim Cause God deeply suffering mankind.

UNIVERSAL HOUSE OF JUSTICE

Message to Bolivia and Mauritius Conferences—August 1970

August 1970

To the Continental Conference in La Paz, Bolivia and the Oceanic Conference in Rose-Hill, Mauritius.

Beloved Friends,

Our hearts turn with eager expectancy to the twin Conferences now in session in the southern hemisphere. Their convocation so shortly after the worldwide commemoration of the Centenary of the Martyrdom of the Purest Branch, calls to mind that the promotion and establishment of the Faith of God have always been through sacrifice and dedicated service. Indeed, these very Conferences testify to the creative power, the fruitfulness, the invocation of Divine confirmations which result from sacrificial service to the Cause of God. Although both Bolivia and Mauritius are mentioned specifically in the tablets of the Divine Plan, the Cause, even thirty-five years ago, was virtually unknown in those areas: today we witness the holding of these historic Conferences.

Little wonder that South America, whose rulers and presidents were addressed by Bahá'u'lláh in His Kitáb-i-Aqdas, of whose indigenous believers the Master, in those Tablets already referred to, wrote ". . . Should these Indians be educated and properly guided, there can be no doubt that through the divine teachings they will become so enlightened that the whole earth will be illumined," should have exerted a magnetic attraction upon a number of ardent souls in the northern continent, eager to serve in so promising a field. A band of heroic pioneers, bearing the Message of Bahá'u'lláh, gradually penetrated its wide territories, its jungles and mountains. They were followed by others under systematic crusades of two Seven-Year Plans and the beloved Guardian's Ten-Year Plan and together they became the spiritual conquerors of that continent. The Latin American communities which arose as a result of their pioneer efforts were described by the beloved Guardian as "associates in the execution" of 'Abdu'l-Bahá's Divine Plan. May Maxwell, one of the great heroines of the Faith, attained her longed-for crown of martyrdom in Buenos Aires; Panama became the site of the sixth Mashriqu'l-Adhkár of the Bahá'í world, and La Paz, Bolivia, is now the scene of this Continental Conference.

The Indian Ocean, whose furthermost waves lap the shores of the Cradle of our Faith, upon whose waters the Divine Báb traveled in the course of His pilgrimage to Mecca, the heart of Islám, where He openly announced His Mission; whose mighty subcontinent from which it derives its name was the home and assigned province of the ninth Letter of the Living; whose major islands were severally mentioned by 'Abdu'l-Bahá in the second of His Tablets of the Divine Plan, lay, for most of a century, fallow to the Word of God, a challenge to the promotion of His Faith. This challenge was answered by half a hundred Knights of Bahá'u'lláh, who, in response to the beloved Guardian's call left their homes and wholeheartedly gave themselves to the establishment of the

Cause in those parts. They implanted the banner of Bahá'u'lláh upon its atolls, its great islands and bordering territories. Now, in the midmost heart of that huge expanse of sea, Mauritius, an island whose name was enshrined in Bahá'í history during the Heroic Age of our Faith as the source, two years before 'Abdu'l-Bahá's arrival in America, of a contribution to the purchase of the site of the Mother Temple of the West, has been chosen as the venue of this oceanic Conference.

Not only have the institutions of the Faith been established in this ocean and this continent, but the spirit of the New Day, brilliant even at this early dawn with the light of Bahá'u'lláh's gifts to man, is apparent in the diversity of the attendants, in the brotherhood of erstwhile strangers—even enemies—and above all in the noble purposes for which you have gathered.

Your aim is the redemption of mankind from its godlessness, its ignorance, its confusion and conflict. You will succeed, as those before you succeeded, by sacrifice to the Cause of God. The deeds and services required of you now, will shine in the future, even as those of your spiritual predecessors shine today and will forever shine in the annals of the Cause.

We share with you the spiritual delight of these occasions and assure you of our constant and ardent prayers that your deliberations upon the objectives of the Cause in your areas and the spiritual fellowship which you will enjoy will result in immediate and determined plans to complete the tasks assigned to you ere the rapidly approaching end of the Nine Year Plan. This Plan is the current stage of the Master's Divine Plan and its success must precede those greater triumphs when, as the result of your labors, the divine outpourings will raise up a vast concourse of radiant and devoted servants of Bahá'u'lláh who will establish His Kingdom in this world.

With loving Bahá'í greetings,
THE UNIVERSAL HOUSE OF JUSTICE

Formation of Seven National Spiritual Assemblies during Riḍván 1971

12 August 1970

To: All National Spiritual Assemblies

Dear Bahá'í Friends,

The following cable has just been sent to Hands of the Cause Rúḥíyyih Khánum and William Sears representing the Universal House of Justice at Conferences in Bolivia and Mauritius:

> Please announce to participants conference joyous news decision call three additional national conventions next Riḍván namely Sudan Chad and Congo Brazzaville Gabon bringing to seven new National Spiritual Assemblies being formed at close of seventh year Nine Year Plan. Fervently praying Holy Shrines behalf national communities Bahá'í world reaching one hundred one by next Riḍván supplicating reinforcement ties uniting them greater consecration challenging tasks still ahead wider participation all ranks faithful. Communicating text cable all National Spiritual Assemblies.

Please share this news with the friends.

With loving Bahá'í greetings,
THE UNIVERSAL HOUSE OF JUSTICE

Grave Crisis in Bahá'í International Fund

29 December 1970

To the Followers of Bahá'u'lláh in every land.

Dear Bahá'í Friends,

We have reached a critical point in the progress of the Nine Year Plan. In many lands multitudes are thirsty and eager to embrace the Message of Bahá'u'lláh. In others, materially advanced but spiritually backward, a great effort is needed to awaken the people to the light of this New Day. The recently established National Spiritual Assemblies in many lands are occupied in acquiring the Ḥaẓíratu'l-Quds, Temple Sites, National Endowments and Teaching Institutes essential for the proper development of the Administrative Order and the deepening of the Bahá'í knowledge of their believers, while in the heart of the Western Hemisphere, the Mashriqu'l-Adhkár of Panama requires several hundred thousand dollars for its completion. To accomplish these many essential tasks the resources of the Cause are being stretched to their uttermost.

At this crucial moment, when the activities of the believers and the expenditure of funds should be increased to seize the opportunities which lie before us, the Bahá'í International Fund finds itself plunged into a grave crisis by a steep reduction in contributions. Undoubtedly worldwide economic difficulties are one of the causes of this, but we are confident that the believers throughout the world will respond to this challenge and will make every sacrifice to ensure that the work of the Cause of God goes forward unimpeded.

Since 1963 when there were 56 National Spiritual Assemblies, to the present time when there are 94 (soon to be 101), the work of the Cause has expanded so rapidly, both in the teaching field and at the World Center, that the Universal House of Justice has had to increase more than fourfold the annual international budget of the Cause. This year fifty-eight percent of the International Fund is being expended outside the Holy Land on projects such as assistance to National Spiritual Assemblies (56 of which receive a large part, if not all, of their budgets from the World Center), contributions to the work of the Hands of the Cause and the Continental Boards of Counselors, defense of the Cause in lands where it is facing persecution, and our expanded activities at the United Nations.

In order to meet the present situation the Universal House of Justice must drastically reduce the expenditure of the Bahá'í International Fund until the flow of contributions is restored. While the work on the International Archives Building necessary to protect the precious Tablets and relics from the high humidity and increasingly polluted atmosphere of Haifa city has been completed, the projects of further developing the Gardens in Bahjí and of starting upon an extension of the Terraces below the Shrine of the Báb, as well as additional developments to the office facilities of the World Center, must now be postponed. In addition we are reluctantly compelled to reduce by ten percent the next two quarterly remittances of assistance to National Spiritual Assemblies, and we call upon these Assemblies now to reduce their own expenditure to take account of this.

These, however, can but be temporary measures designed to minimize the present emergency. The real answer lies, not in restricting the activities of the friends at this time when mankind stands in such dire need of the Message of Bahá'u'lláh, but in the universal participation of every believer in the work of the Cause.

The poor believers vastly outnumber the wealthy ones, and this majority will grow rapidly as mass teaching spreads. Thus, although the work in mass teaching areas will continue to be assisted by the contributions of the friends in prosperous lands, and these believers must for the immediate future continue to be the main support of the International Fund, it becomes ever more urgent for the friends in mass teaching areas to finance their own activities to an ever greater degree. The backbone of the Fund must be the regular contributions of every believer. Even though such contributions may be small because of the poverty of the donors, large numbers of small sums combine into a mighty river that can carry along the work of the Cause. Moreover the unity of the friends in sacrifice draws upon them the confirmations of the Blessed Beauty.

The universal participation of the believers in every aspect of the Faith—in contributing to the Fund, in teaching, deepening, living the Bahá'í life, administering the affairs of the community, and, above all, in the life of prayer and devotion to God—will endow the Bahá'í community with such strength that it can overcome the forces of spiritual disintegration which are engulfing the non-Bahá'í world, and can become an ocean of oneness that will cover the face of the planet.

We ask every one of you to ponder these matters deeply, and to join us in fervent prayer that this momentary crisis will prove to have been a providential test that will spur the community of the Greatest Name to new heights of dedication and triumphant achievement.

With loving Bahá'í greetings,
THE UNIVERSAL HOUSE OF JUSTICE

Crisis in Bahá'í Fund in United States

29 December 1970

To the Believers in the Cradle of the
Bahá'í Administrative Order.

Dear Bahá'í Friends,

Your National Spiritual Assembly is, at this very time, taking urgent steps to acquaint each one of you with the serious condition of your National Fund, and we are sure that, as soon as you know of this situation, you will respond with the generosity and self-sacrifice that are characteristic of the American Bahá'í community.

The crisis in your National Fund has, in its turn, precipitated a crisis in the international funds of the Cause, because your National Spiritual Assembly has been unable to send more than a small proportion of the $600,000 which it had decided to contribute to the International Fund. The inability of your National Assembly to transmit this contribution to the Holy Land has caused us to drastically reduce expenditures in the international work of the Cause, as explained in the letter to the friends throughout the world, which is enclosed.

As the United States' own mass teaching progresses, your National Fund will have to be expended increasingly on vital deepening and consolidation projects, for it is important that the new believers who are entering the community in such large numbers be rapidly integrated into the life of the whole. The administration of the Cause in the United States is entering a completely new phase, of high promise, challenging problems and golden opportunities. You are the cradle of the Administration, and in this development too you can become a pattern for the entire Bahá'í world. The essential requirement at this time is complete unity and whole-hearted support for your National Spiritual Assembly, both in action and in funds.

Once again, the progress of the Cause throughout the world hangs largely on the response and single-minded devotion of the American followers of Bahá'u'lláh. That they may arise with characteristic youthful fervor and trust in Almighty God is our ardent prayer at the Sacred Threshold.

> With loving Bahá'í greetings,
> THE UNIVERSAL HOUSE OF JUSTICE

Message to the Monrovia Conference—January 1971

January 1971

Dearly-loved Friends,

The emergence on the African Continent of a widely spread, numerous, diversified and united Bahá'í community, so swiftly after the initiation of organized teaching plans there, is of the utmost significance and a signal evidence of the bounties which God has destined for its peoples in this day.

The great victories in Africa, which brought such joy to the Guardian's heart in the last years of his life, resulted from the self-sacrificing devotion of a handful of pioneers, gradually assisted by the first few native believers, all laboring under the loving shadow of the Hand of the Cause Músá Banání. From their efforts there has been raised up an increasing army of African teachers, administrators, pioneers and valiant promoters of the Divine Cause, whose main task is to bring to all Africa the bounties conferred by the Word of God, bounties of enlightenment, zeal, devotion and eventually the true civilization of Bahá'u'lláh's World Order.

Many of the gravest ills now afflicting the human race appear in acute form on the African Continent. Racial, tribal and religious prejudice, disunity of nations, the scourge of political factionalism, poverty and lack of education are obvious examples. Bahá'ís have a great part to play—greater than they may realize—in the healing of these sicknesses and the abatement of their worst effects. By their radiant unity, by their "bright and shining" faces, their self-discipline in zealously following all the requirements of Bahá'í law, their abstention from politics, their constant study and proclamation of the Great Message, they will hasten the advent of that glorious day when all mankind will know its true brotherhood and will bask in the sunshine of God's love and blessing.

That the African believers are fully capable of taking their full share in building the Kingdom of God on earth, their natural abilities and present deeds have fully demonstrated. An African Hand of the Cause of God, even now in the course of a brilliant, triumphal teaching tour of the planet, African Counselors, Board Members, national and local administrators and an ever-increasing army of believers testify to the vigor and immense capacity of this highly-blessed continent to serve its Lord in the great day of His appearance. That the African believers, so beloved by the Guardian of the Faith, will rise to the challenge facing them and earn the gratitude and goodwill of all mankind by their deeds of dedication and self-sacrifice is the longing of our hearts.

May this Conference become a sun from which will stream forth to all parts of the vast continent rays of spiritual energy and inspiration, galvanizing the friends to action in the fields of teaching and pioneering in such manner that they will rapidly achieve all the tasks assigned to them under the Nine Year Plan.

Our thoughts and prayers are with you.

THE UNIVERSAL HOUSE OF JUSTICE

Message to the Oceanic Conference of the South China Seas, Singapore—January 1971

January 1971

Dearly-loved Friends,

The wonderful progress made by the Bahá'í communities of South East Asia towards achievement of the tasks assigned to them under the Nine Year Plan, fills our hearts with thankfulness to God and arouses our keenest admiration for the capacities and dedicated services of the friends in all those vast and varied territories. Indeed, so bountiful have been the divine confirmations rewarding their efforts that we are confident of their ability to far exceed the stated objectives and to initiate the opening phase of the next stage of their development, a massive increase in the establishment of the Cause of God among the teeming millions of the islands and ocean-bordering countries of so huge an area of the earth.

South East Asia, whose gifted and industrious peoples have embraced four of the world's major religions, have produced in all ages civilizations and cultures representative of the highest accomplishments of the human race, now experiencing with the rest of the world the disruptive, revolutionizing, "vibrating influence of this Most Great, this New World Order, the like of which mortal eyes have never witnessed," lies open and receptive to the Word of God, ready once more to nourish in its fertile soil that potent seed and to bring forth, in its own characteristic manner and as an integral part of the world civilization, the institutions, the fabric, the brilliant edifice of Bahá'u'lláh's World Order.

We now summon the believers of this highly-promising area, flushed with the tide of approaching victory, to launch a three-pronged campaign, the main feature of which is to achieve an immediate expansion of the Faith, exceeding the aims of the Nine Year Plan. In addition you are called upon to raise a corps of traveling teachers, whose main objective will be to visit all the communities and groups in the area for the purpose of deepening and consolidating their Bahá'í life, thus preserving the victories won and reinforcing the base for future development. Simultaneously a number of Chinese-speaking believers must arise who, as pioneers and traveling teachers in all the countries of South East Asia, will attract large numbers of the talented Chinese race to embrace and serve the Faith of Bahá'u'lláh.

Recognizing your current achievements and fully confident in your determination and ability to continue to attract the divine confirmations of Bahá'u'lláh, we are happy to announce as a supplementary goal of the Nine Year Plan, the establishment, at Riḍván, 1972, of the National Spiritual

Assembly of the Bahá'ís of Singapore, an additional supporting pillar of the Universal House of Justice and a new bastion of the Faith in so vital a crossroads of human activity.

We pray that your deliberations will engender a new wave of enthusiasm, cement ever more firmly the bonds of love between the many and various national communities of your area and result in practical plans for the implementation of the above tasks.

We send you all our most loving greetings and look forward eagerly to the report of your conference.

THE UNIVERSAL HOUSE OF JUSTICE

Acceleration of Enrollments in the United States

31 January 1971

To: All National Spiritual Assemblies

Dear Bahá'í Friends,

We share with you the text of a cable sent today to the National Spiritual Assembly of the United States for publication in "*Bahá'í News*":

Joyfully announce Bahá'í world process entry by troops rapidly accelerating United States evidenced by enrollment 8000 new believers South Carolina course six weeks campaign raising number new believers entire country 13000 since Riḍván. Process gathering momentum. Indications similar development occurring new areas North South America. May valiant workers Faith toiling throughout world gain confidence added strength these uplifting victories won in His name reap similar harvest homefronts all continents (Signed) Universal House of Justice.

With loving Bahá'í greetings,
THE UNIVERSAL HOUSE OF JUSTICE

Participation of the Hands of the Cause of God in First National Conventions

1 February 1971

To: All National Spiritual Assemblies

Dear Bahá'í Friends,

We share with you the text of a cable sent today to the National Spiritual Assembly of the United States for publication in "Bahá'í News":

Please publish Bahá'í News following happy announce following Hands Cause will represent Universal House Justice first national conventions coming Riḍván Amatu'l-Bahá Rúḥíyyih Khánum Ivory Coast Upper Volta Mali Dhikr'u'lláh Khadem Trinidad Tobago Adelbert Muhlschlegel Lesotho 'Alí Muḥammad Varqá Congo Brazzaville Gabon Enoch Olinga both Sudan Chad Collis Featherstone both Solomon Islands Southwest Pacific Ocean. Confident presence participation these standard bearers Nine Year Plan historic first conventions will attract divine blessings assist new national communities befittingly assume sacred responsibilities (signed) Universal House of Justice.

With loving Bahá'í greetings,
THE UNIVERSAL HOUSE OF JUSTICE

Formation of Nine Additional National Spiritual Assemblies during Riḍván 1972

11 February 1971

To: All National Spiritual Assemblies

Dear Bahá'í Friends,

We share with you the text of a cable sent today to the National Spiritual Assembly of the United States for publication in "Bahá'í News":

Please publish Bahá'í News following rejoice announce all friends formation during Riḍván 1972 nine additional National Spiritual Assemblies raising total number pillars Universal House Justice to one hundred and ten. Three in Africa Malagasy Republic Réunion Seychelles three in Asia East Pakistan Nepal Singapore one in Australasia Northwest Pacific Ocean comprising Guam Carolines Marianas Marshalls two in Europe Iceland and Republic Ireland. Four of these Seychelles East Pakistan Singapore Northwest Pacific constitute supplementary achievements Nine Year Plan. Urge pioneers scheduled all these areas settle posts without delay. Call upon respective communities brace themselves exert supreme effort fast fleeting weeks before coming Riḍván establish as many Assemblies as possible thereby broadening strengthening foundations projected national institutions. Fervently praying Holy Shrines followers Most Great Name may seize unique opportunities present hour and spare no effort until goals Plan are fully accomplished thereby attracting to themselves and their communities inestimable blessings Ancient Beauty (Signed) Universal House of Justice.

> With loving Bahá'í greetings,
> THE UNIVERSAL HOUSE OF JUSTICE

Warning against the Misuse of Recordings of 'Abdu'l-Bahá's Voice

23 February 1971

To: All National Spiritual Assemblies

Dear Bahá'í Friends,

The advent and liberal supply of tape and cassette recorders in the markets of the world have opened new doors and placed in almost every land at the disposal of the friends new methods for the dissemination of Bahá'í material. It is the hope of the

Universal House of Justice that the recording of Bahá'í talks, and other audio features, and their wide use among Bahá'ís and non-Bahá'ís alike, will prove to be a powerful new instrument in the teaching and deepening work everywhere. There is one area, however, where great care must be exercised, and this is the use of the record of 'Abdu'l-Bahá's voice.

The Guardian, when referring to this record, requested the friends "to exercise restraint and caution." "In my view," he added, "it should be used only on special occasions and be listened to with the utmost reverence. The dignity of the Cause, I am sure, would suffer from too wide and indiscriminate use of one of the most precious relics of our departed Master."

We request you to share the contents of this letter, in any manner you deem advisable, with the friends residing under your jurisdiction. We are confident that all the friends will strictly observe the Guardian's exhortation and will not overstep the bounds of courtesy and moderation in the use of a precious relic so lovingly left to us by the Center of God's Covenant.

With loving Bahá'í greetings,
THE UNIVERSAL HOUSE OF JUSTICE

Riḍván Message 1971

Riḍván 1971

To the Bahá'ís of the World

Dearly-loved Friends,

On November 28th 1971 the Bahá'í World will commemorate the fiftieth anniversary of the Passing of 'Abdu'l-Bahá, the Center of the Covenant, the Ensign of the Oneness of Mankind, the Mystery of God, an event which signalized at once the end of the Heroic Age of our Faith, the opening of the Formative Age and the birth of the Administrative Order, the nucleus and pattern of the World Order of Bahá'u'lláh. As we contemplate the fruits of the Master's Ministry harvested during the first fifty years of the Formative Age, a period dominated by the dynamic and beloved figure of Shoghi Effendi, whose life was dedicated to the systematic implementation of the provisions of the Will and Testament of 'Abdu'l-Bahá and of the Tablets of the Divine Plan—the two charters provided by the Master for the administration and the teaching of the Cause of God—we may well experience a sense of awe at the prospect of the next fifty years. That first half-century of the Formative Age has seen the Bahá'í Community grow from a few hundred centers in 35 countries in 1921, to over 46,000 centers in 135 independent states and 182 significant territories and islands at the present day, has been marked by the raising throughout the world of the framework of the Administrative Order, which in its turn has brought recognition of the Faith by many governments and civil authorities and accreditation in consultative status to the Economic and Social Council of the United Nations, and has witnessed the spread to many parts of the world of that "entry by troops" promised by the Master and so long and so eagerly anticipated by the friends.

A new horizon, bright with intimations of thrilling developments in the unfolding life of the Cause of God, is now discernible. The approach to it is complete victory in the Nine Year Plan. For we should never forget that the beloved Guardian's Ten Year Crusade, the current Nine Year Plan, other plans to follow throughout successive epochs of the Formative Age of the Faith, are all phases in the implementation of the Divine Plan of 'Abdu'l-Bahá, set out in fourteen of His Tablets to North America.

The Nine Year Plan is well advanced, and this Riḍván will witness the establishment of seven more National Spiritual Assemblies, five in Africa, one in South America and one in the Pacific, bringing the total number of these exalted bodies to 101. Next Riḍván the nine already announced will be formed, together with 4 more, one each in Afghanistan, Arabia, the Windward Islands and Puerto Rico, bringing the total to 114, six more than called for in the Nine Year Plan. The members of all National Spiritual Assemblies which will be elected at Riḍván 1972 will take part in the election of the Universal House of Justice at Riḍván 1973, when an international convention will be held at the World Center.

The Mother Temple of Latin America, the Mashriqu'l-Adhkár of Panama, is scheduled to be completed by December 1971, and its dedication will take place at the following Riḍván.

The wonderful spirit released at the four Oceanic and Intercontinental Conferences, together with the practical benefits which accrued to the Cause from them, reinforce our high hopes that the four Conferences to be held this year will be resounding successes and result in more pioneers, more traveling teachers, greater proclamation of the Message and a raising of the spirits and devotion of the friends.

Our appeal to the friends in December 1970 for support of the Bahá'í International Fund, which had reached a serious condition due to various unforeseen circumstances, has had a magnificent response from many quarters of the worldwide Bahá'í Community, and we are heartened to believe that this manifestation of devotion and sacrifice, as it continues and becomes more widespread, will resolve the condition that had threatened to adversely affect the attainment of cherished goals of the Nine Year Plan.

The travels and other services of the Hands of the Cause of God continually evoke our thankfulness and delight, even wonder and astonishment. Their deeds are such as to eclipse the acts of the apostles of old and to confer eternal splendor on this period of the Formative Age. On behalf of all the friends everywhere, we offer them our reverent love and gratitude. It is fitting to record here the passing, after seventy years exemplary service to the Faith, of the Hand of the Cause Agnes

Alexander, whose early services in Hawaii were said by the Master to be greater than if she had founded an empire.

Restrictive measures, directed against the Faith, and varying in severity from outright oppression to imposition of disabilities make virtually impossible the achievement of the goals of the Nine Year Plan in a number of countries, particularly in the Middle East, in North West Africa, along the fringes of East Africa and certain areas in South East Asia. It is hoped that those Bahá'í communities which enjoy freedom to teach their Faith will so far surpass their own goals as to amply compensate for the disabilities suffered by their less fortunate brothers. The army of traveling teachers must be reinforced and the friends, particularly Bahá'í youth, are called to seriously consider how much time they can offer to the Faith during the remaining two years of the Nine Year Plan. Teaching visits of brief or long duration, deputization of others, the undertaking of such tasks as would free other friends for teaching work, are all means of building up, in unison, that final surge which will carry the Plan to victory.

Two major objectives of the Plan are the formation of new Local Spiritual Assemblies and the opening of new localities. 13,996 Local Spiritual Assemblies are called for; 10,360 are now in existence. 54,503 localities must claim a Bahá'í resident; 46,334 do so now. The goal is in sight, the time short. However, the growth reflected in the above statistics has not taken place at all levels and in all areas. For while a number of national communities have already achieved, or even surpassed the goals assigned to them, many face extreme difficulties in attaining theirs. With mutual help and an increase in the momentum already generated there is no doubt that the community of the Most Great Name is capable of sweeping on to total victory, thereby gaining a view of those enthralling vistas at present beyond the horizon.

The twin processes so clearly described by the beloved Guardian in his essay "The Unfoldment of World

Civilization"—the steady progress and consolidation of the Cause of God on the one hand and the progressive disintegration of a moribund world on the other—will undoubtedly impose upon us new tasks, the obligation of devising new approaches to teaching, of demonstrating more clearly to a disillusioned world the Bahá'í way of life and making more effective the administrative institutions of the Faith. The authority and influence of National and Local Spiritual Assemblies will have to be strengthened in order to deal with larger Bahá'í communities; the international character of the Cause will need to be developed, while the international teaching agency at the World Center, already referred to in previous general letters, will be established.

However fascinating such considerations, which are likely to be forced upon our attention in the near future, may be, they must not deflect our energies and will from the immediate task—the goals of the Nine Year Plan. Their achievement is the best preparation for the future and the means of developing new powers and capacities in the Bahá'í Community. We are confident that the Army of Light, growing in strength and unity will, by 1973, the centenary year of the revelation of the Kitáb-i-Aqdas, have scaled the heights of yet another peak in the path leading ultimately to the broad uplands of the Most Great Peace.

> With loving Bahá'í greetings,
> THE UNIVERSAL HOUSE OF JUSTICE

Message to the Caribbean Conference—May 1971

May 1971

To the Friends of God gathered in the Caribbean Conference

Warmest greetings!

How propitious that on its mountaintop between the two greatest oceans and the two American continents the Mother

Temple of Latin America is rising now in Panama, a land blessed by 'Abdu'l-Bahá's prophecy that "in the future it will gain great importance." How splendid that the vision projected in the Divine Plan for the Americas has sprung into such vibrant life in this Caribbean basin, in country after country upon its verdant shores, in island after island across its expanse, all named by the Master in His Tablets. What shall we not witness erelong in these places so charged with destiny through the Master's utterances!

The Nine Year Plan, the current stage in the unfoldment of the Divine Plan of 'Abdu'l-Bahá, is approaching its triumphant end. This Conference is an occasion to sum up what has been won, to determine to achieve the remaining goals for expansion in these blessed lands, and to consolidate the old and new communities of the Most Great Name. Indeed, the winning of our grand Bahá'í objectives began just yesterday when, in the early years of the Formative Age, a few travelers crossed the Caribbean. Yet it was not until the successive Plans of the beloved Guardian, culminating in the Ten Year Crusade, when 27 Knights of Bahá'u'lláh settled throughout this vast area, that the Cause took firm root. By 1963 the countries and islands of the Caribbean claimed less than 400 localities and only 147 Local Spiritual Assemblies. Now Bahá'ís are to be found in over 2,500 localities, more than 500 Local Assemblies and 16 National Spiritual Assemblies have been formed, and there have been hundreds of concrete achievements which have brought about our recognition as an independent Faith.

The Americas have been a melting pot and a meeting place for the races of men, and the need is acute for the fulfillment of God's promises of the realization of the oneness of mankind. Particularly do the Master and the Guardian point to the Afro-Americans and the Amerindians, two great ethnic groups whose spiritual powers will be released through their response to the Creative Word. But our Teachings must touch all, must include all peoples. And, in this hour of your tireless activity, what special rewards shall come to those who will arise, summoned by 'Abdu'l-Bahá's Words: "Now is the time to divest yourselves of the garment of attachment to this phenomenal realm, be wholly severed from the physical world, become angels of heaven, and travel and teach through all these regions."

The time is short, the needs many. No effort can be foregone, no opportunity wasted. Praised be God that you have gathered in this Conference to consult upon the vital requirements of this highly significant moment. Our prayers ascend at the Holy Threshold that every session of this historic meeting will attract Divine Blessings, and that each soul, armed with the love of God and imbued with His purpose for a struggling mankind, will arise to activate, beyond all present hope, the vast spiritual potentialities of the Americas.

To each of you we send our deepest love.

THE UNIVERSAL HOUSE OF JUSTICE

Message to the South Pacific Oceanic Conference—May 1971

May 1971

To the Friends of God Assembled in the
    Conference of the South Pacific Ocean:

Dearly Loved Friends,

We send our warmest greetings and deepest love on the occasion of the first Conference in the heart of the Pacific Ocean. Praised be to God that you have gathered to consult on the vital needs of the hour!

Recalling the promise of Bahá'u'lláh "Should they attempt to conceal His light on the continent, He will assuredly rear

His head in the midmost part of the ocean and, raising His voice proclaim: 'I am the lifegiver of the world!' " we now witness its fulfillment in the vast area of the Pacific Ocean, in island after island mentioned by the Master in the Tablets of the Divine Plan. How great is the potential for the Faith in localities blessed by these references!

At the inception of the Formative Age, the Cause was little known here. Agnes Alexander had brought the Teachings to the Hawaiian Islands. Father and Mother Dunn had only recently arrived in Australia. Later the name of Martha Root was to be emblazoned across the Pacific. Still later, at the beginning of the Ten Year Crusade, a vanguard of twenty-one Knights of Bahá'u'lláh raised His call as they settled in the islands of this great Ocean. The names of these valiant souls, together with the names of the army of pioneers and teachers who followed, will be forever enshrined in the annals of the Faith.

Their mighty endeavors brought about the enrollment of thousands of the peoples of Polynesia, Micronesia and Melanesia under the banner of the Most Great Name, the opening in Australasia of more than 800 centers and the establishment of ten pillars of the Universal House of Justice. We can but marvel at such triumphs attained despite great difficulties imposed by the vast expanses of ocean separating the island communities, especially when it is recalled that in many of these islands even the Christian Gospel was unknown as late as the 1880s.

How great is the responsibility to continue spreading the Word of God throughout the Pacific. It was in the Tablets of the Divine Plan that 'Abdu'l-Bahá called for teachers "speaking the languages, severed, holy, sanctified and filled with the love of God," to "turn their faces to and travel through the three great island groups of the Pacific Ocean—Polynesia, Micronesia and Melanesia . . . with hearts overflowing with the love of God, with tongues commemorating the mention of God" to "deliver the Glad Tidings of the manifestation of the Lord of Hosts to all the people."

The Nine Year Plan, the current phase of the unfoldment of the Divine Plan, is now approaching its final stages. It is incumbent on the friends to assess what has been accomplished and to anticipate and plan for such rapid acceleration of the teaching and consolidation work as is necessary to win all goals by 1973. Time is short; the needs critical. No effort must be spared; no opportunity overlooked.

Our prayers ascend at the Holy Threshold that every session of this historic meeting will attract Divine blessings, and that the friends will go forth, armed with the love of God and enthusiasm born of the Spirit, fully prepared to scale the heights of victory!

With loving Bahá'í greetings,
THE UNIVERSAL HOUSE OF JUSTICE

Commemoration of the Fiftieth Anniversary of the Passing of 'Abdu'l-Bahá

12 July 1971

To All National Spiritual Assemblies

Dear Bahá'í Friends,

We have noted with deep satisfaction that some National Spiritual Assemblies have already initiated plans to befittingly commemorate the Fiftieth Anniversary of the passing of 'Abdu'l-Bahá and the inception of the Formative Age of the Bahá'í Dispensation.

We feel it would be highly fitting for the three days, November 26 to 28, during which the Day of the Covenant and the Anniversary of the Ascension of 'Abdu'l-Bahá occur, to be set aside this year by all National Spiritual Assemblies for specially arranged gatherings and conferences, convened either nationally or locally or both, on the three following main themes: The Bahá'í Covenant, The Formative Age, and The Life of 'Abdu'l-Bahá.

We hope that these gatherings will serve to intensify the consecration of the workers in the Divine Vineyard in every land, and provide them with the opportunity, especially in the watches of the night of that Ascension, when they will be commemorating the passing hour of our Beloved Master, to renew their pledge to Bahá'u'lláh and to rededicate themselves to the accomplishment of the as yet unfulfilled goals of the Nine Year Plan.

The Hands of the Cause in the Holy Land, the members of the Universal House of Justice, and all resident and visiting believers at the World Center will, on that memory-laden night, visit the Shrine of that Mystery of God on behalf of the entire Community of the Blessed Beauty and will supplicate for the stalwart champions of the Faith laboring in the forefront of so many fields of service and winning fresh triumphs in His Name, for the self-sacrificing believers without whose support and sustained assistance most of these victories could not be achieved, and for those who will be inspired to join the ranks of the active and dedicated promoters of His glorious Cause at this crucial stage in the development of the Plan, that we may all meet our obligations and discharge our sacred trust, thus making it possible in the latter months of the Plan for our entire resources to be devoted to an even greater expansion of the Faith in its onward march towards the spiritual conquest of the planet.

With loving Bahá'í greetings,
THE UNIVERSAL HOUSE OF JUSTICE

Message to the North Pacific
Oceanic Conference—September 1971

September 1971

To the Friends of God Assembled in the
 Conference of the North Pacific Ocean

Dearly-loved Friends,

On the eve of the Fiftieth Anniversary of the opening of the Formative Age of our Faith we call to mind the high hopes often expressed by the beloved Master for the spread of the Cause in this region, His mention in the Tablets of the Divine Plan of many of the territories represented in this Conference, and the faithful and devoted services of that maidservant of Bahá'u'lláh, the Hand of the Cause Agnes Alexander, who brought the Teachings to these shores in the early years of this century.

In these days we are witnessing an unprecedented acceleration of the teaching work in almost every part of the globe. In the North Pacific Ocean area great strides have been made in the advancement of the Cause since that historic Asia Regional Teaching Conference in Nikko just sixteen years ago. The next two years witnessed the formation of the National Spiritual Assembly of Alaska and of the Regional National Spiritual Assembly of North East Asia. To the Convention in Tokyo at Riḍván 1957 the Guardian addressed these prophetic words:

This auspicious event, which posterity will regard as the culmination of a process initiated, half a century ago, in the capital city of Japan . . . marks the opening of the second chapter in the history of the evolution of His Faith in the North Pacific area. Such a consummation cannot fail to lend a tremendous impetus to its onward march in the entire Pacific Ocean . . .

Since that time National Spiritual Assemblies have also been firmly established in Korea and Taiwan.

Hokkaido, the site of this Conference, first heard of the Teachings less than fifteen years ago, and the first aboriginal peoples of this land accepted Bahá'u'lláh just over a decade ago. Now you are the witnesses to the beginnings of a rapid increase in the number of believers. Peoples in other islands and lands of the North Pacific, including the Ryukyus, Guam, the Trust Territories, the western shores of Canada and Alaska and the Aleutians are also enrolling under the banner of the Most Great Name, the next Riḍván yet another pillar of the Universal House of Justice is to be raised in Micronesia. We are heartened at the prospect that from the indigenous peoples of this vast oceanic area, the Ainu, the Japanese, the Chinese, the Koreans, the Okinawans, the Micronesians, the American Indians, the Eskimos, and the Aleuts vast numbers will soon enter the Faith.

The final hours of the Nine Year Plan are fast fleeting. Praised be to God that you have gathered to consult on ways and means of assuring complete victory so that from these outposts the teachings may spread to those nearby lands where teeming millions have not as yet heard of the advent of this Most Great Dispensation.

The sweet perfume of victory is in the air, and we must hasten to achieve it while there is yet time. Vital goals, particularly on the homefronts of Taiwan and Japan, remain to be won, and everywhere the roots of the faith of the believers must sink deeper and deeper into the firm earth of the Teachings lest tempests and trials as yet unforeseen shake or uproot the tender plants so lovingly raised in the islands of this great Ocean and the lands surrounding it.

As you and the friends in the sister Conference in Reykjavik bring this series of eight Oceanic and Continental Conferences to a triumphant close, our prayers for the success of your deliberations ascend at the Holy Threshold. May God grant you the resources, the strength, and the determination to attain your highest hopes, and enable you to open a new and glorious chapter in the evolution of His Faith in the North Pacific area.

> With loving Bahá'í greetings,
> THE UNIVERSAL HOUSE OF JUSTICE

Message to the North Atlantic Conference—September 1971

September 1971

To the Friends Assembled in the
  North Atlantic Conference in Reykjavik

Dearly-loved Friends,

To each and every one of you in this historic Conference we send our most cordial and loving greetings. The famous island in which you are now gathered, so strategically placed between the two great continents flanking the vast oceanic area which surrounds it, to which the Teachings of Christ were brought a millennium ago, and which, in this Dispensation, was mentioned by the Center of the Covenant in His Tablets of the Divine Plan, first heard the Name of Bahá'u'lláh in 1924 when the Hand of the Cause Amelia Collins stopped briefly in Reykjavik and made the acquaintance of Hólmfríður Arnadóttir who subsequently became the first Bahá'í of Iceland. Eleven years later the beloved Martha Root spent a month in this land which she loved so well. On that occasion, with the help of Hólmfríður, the Cause of Bahá'u'lláh was widely proclaimed in the press, on the radio and from the lecture platform.

The great Ocean extending from the equator to the Pole and from Europe to North America, which has been both the barrier and the link between the Old and the New Worlds, has played a highly significant part in the later history of mankind. Long before Columbus arrived in the West Indies the Vikings, forebears of Icelanders of today, were plying its northern waters. In later centuries wave upon wave of Europeans sailed from east to west, engaging in one of the most significant migrations in human history. In the twentieth century 'Abdu'l-Bahá Himself sailed across it and back, a voyage unique in the religious history of mankind and creating a remarkable parallel with the Light of the Cause itself, beaming from the East across the great Ocean to the heart of the North American Continent, being reflected back again, firing new beacon lights in Europe and in later years diffusing its radiance throughout the world. The great Republic whose eastern shore forms part of the boundary of this Ocean has become the Cradle of the Administrative Order and at this present time the banner of the Most Great Name is being raised in island after island of this Ocean, two of which—Iceland and Ireland —will raise, next Riḍván, new pillars of the Universal House of Justice.

The Faith of God is flourishing in the lands around the North Atlantic; a new wind is blowing, promoting an upsurge of proclamation and teaching. In Europe the youth are afire with enthusiasm and vigor. In Canada and the United States a ground swell of unknown proportions is carrying Bahá'í communities to heights of unprecedented achievement.

You are gathered in this Conference to consult on ways and means of winning, in the few fleeting months ahead, the remaining goals of the Nine Year Plan. In Europe particularly there is much to be done, but we have full faith that the friends, galvanized by their love for Bahá'u'lláh and fortified by His promises of Divine assistance, will, with the enthusiasm which they already display, commit their resources to the tasks ahead and will surely attain the victory.

The beloved Master prayed that holy souls would arise from the Northern Territories of the West and become signs of God's guidance and standards of the Supreme Concourse. In one of the Tablets of the Divine Plan He refers to an inhospitable island of that area saying:

> Should the fire of the love of God be kindled in Greenland all the ice of that country will be melted, and its cold weather become temperate—that is, if the hearts be touched with the heat of the love of God, that territory will become a divine rose garden and a heavenly paradise, and the souls, even as fruitful trees, will acquire the utmost freshness and beauty. Effort, the utmost effort is required.

As the friends gathered in Reykjavik and Sapporo bring this worldwide series of Oceanic and Continental Conferences to a triumphant close our thoughts are with you and our prayers on your behalf rise from the Sacred Threshold. May untold blessings and confirmations be showered upon you as you go forth to labor for the advancement of the Cause of God and may your brows be crowned with victory.

THE UNIVERSAL HOUSE OF JUSTICE

Formation of Thirteen New National Spiritual Assemblies during Riḍván 1972

7 December 1971

To All National Spiritual Assemblies

Dear Bahá'í Friends,

We share with you the text of a cable sent on December 7th

to the National Spiritual Assembly of the United States for publication in "Bahá'í News":

Please publish Bahá'í News following happy announce decision add Rwanda list National Spiritual Assemblies to be formed next Riḍván. Representatives House Justice first conventions as follows Hands Cause Amatu'l-Bahá Rúḥíyyih Khánum Windward Islands Ugo Giachery Puerto Rico 'Alí-Akbar Furútan Nepal Shu'á'u'lláh 'Alá'í East Pakistan Adelbert Muhlschlegel Rwanda Seychelles Jalál Kházeh Singapore Enoch Olinga Iceland William Sears Ireland Collis Featherstone Northwest Pacific Raḥmatu'lláh Muhájir Malagasy Republic Réunion Counselor Hádí Raḥmaní Afganistan. Praying Shrines outstanding success these historic gatherings electing members new pillars House Justice focal centers spiritual invigoration illumination newly emerging national communities (signed) Universal House of Justice.

> With loving Bahá'í greetings,
> THE UNIVERSAL HOUSE OF JUSTICE

Developments of Properties at the World Center

19 December 1971

To: All National Spiritual Assemblies

Dear Bahá'í Friends,

We share with you the following text of a cable which has been sent to the National Spiritual Assembly of the United States:

Joyously announce further developments World Center. After many years difficult negotiations erection obelisk marking site future Mashriqu'l-Adhkár Mount Carmel completed thus fulfilling project initiated beloved Guardian early years crusade. Gardens Bahjí Haifa extended by development quadrant southeast Mansion Bahá'u'lláh and establishment formal garden southwest corner property surrounding Shrine Báb.

> With loving Bahá'í greetings,
> THE UNIVERSAL HOUSE OF JUSTICE

Announcement That Number of Localities Exceeds Nine Year Plan Goal

14 February 1972

To All National Spiritual Assemblies

Dear Bahá'í Friends,

We share with you the text of a cable sent on February 14th to the National Spiritual Assembly of the United States for publication in "Bahá'í News":

Please publish Bahá'í News following overjoyed announce friends every land number localities now 56645 exceeding by over 2500 original goal Nine Year Plan. Offering prayers thanksgiving Sacred Threshold for divine bounties surrounding sacrificial efforts love intoxicated supporters His blessed name. Urge believers those areas whose teaching goals are still outstanding exert utmost effort course swiftly passing remaining months Plan win their goals enabling them join ranks their victorious brethren who are urged continue their vigorous brilliant exploits in service God's infinitely glorious Cause (signed) Universal House of Justice.

> With loving Bahá'í greetings,
> THE UNIVERSAL HOUSE OF JUSTICE

Comments on the Semiannual
Statistical Report of the United States

14 February 1972

National Spiritual Assembly of the
Bahá'ís of the United States

Dear Bahá'í Friends,

We were delighted with the information contained in your semiannual statistical report. The believers in the United States are to be applauded for opening, during the past six-month period, 642 localities to the Faith and enrolling 3,053 believers.

We note that the new teaching methods you have developed, in reaching the waiting masses, have substantially influenced the winning of your goals, and we urge the American Bahá'ís, one and all, newly enrolled and believers of long standing, to arise, put their reliance in Bahá'u'lláh and armed with that supreme power, continue unabated their efforts to reach the waiting souls, while simultaneously consolidating the hard-won victories. New methods inevitably bring with them criticism and challenges no matter how successful they may ultimately prove to be. The influx of so many new believers is, in itself, a call to the veteran believers to join the ranks of those in this field of service and to give wholeheartedly of their knowledge and experience. Far from standing aloof, the American believers are called upon now, as never before, to grasp this golden opportunity which has been presented to them, to consult together prayerfully and widen the scope of their endeavors.

Efforts to reach the minorities should be increased and broadened to include all minority groups such as the Indians,

Spanish-speaking people, Japanese and Chinese. Indeed, every stratum of American society must be reached and can be reached with the healing Message, if the believers will but arise and go forth with the spirit which is conquering the citadels of the southern states. Such a program, coupled as it must be with continuous consolidation, can be effectively carried out by universal participation on the part of every lover of Bahá'u'lláh.

Your goals are well-nigh won and you have only to form one Local Assembly in Bermuda and one in the Falkland Islands. You must pursue your efforts to translate and publish literature in Kazakh and enrich literature for the Indians. The palm of victory is within your reach.

We shall continue to pray fervently at the Holy Shrines for the self-sacrificing labors of the beloved friends in the United States.

> With loving Bahá'í greetings,
> THE UNIVERSAL HOUSE OF JUSTICE

Message on the Occasion of the Dedication of the Panama Temple

19 March 1972

To the Beloved of God gathered in the
  Conference called on the occasion of the
  Dedication of the Mother Temple of Latin America

Dear Bahá'í Friends,

With praise and gratitude to God the whole Bahá'í world acclaims the dedication of the Mother Temple of Latin America, an edifice which glorifies the Cause of Bahá'u'lláh at that point where, the beloved Master asserted, "the Occident and the Orient find each other united through the Panama Canal," where "the teachings, once established . . . , will unite the East and the West, the North and the South."

This historic project, in a hemisphere of infinite spiritual potentiality, fulfills one of the most important goals of the Nine Year Plan, and brings untold joy to the hearts of the friends in every land. Privileged are they who shared in the raising of this glorious Silent Teacher with deeds of loving generosity and sacrifice. A crown to the labors of all those who have striven to establish the Faith of Bahá'u'lláh in Latin America, this Mashriqu'l-Adhkár, the rallying point for the Bahá'ís of those lands, whether they are of the blessed Indian peoples or represent the other races whose diversity enriches the nations of that hemisphere, will be a fountainhead of spiritual confirmations, and this mighty achievement will endow the Bahá'í Community with new and greater capacities, enabling the friends in Latin America, and particularly in this privileged land of Panama, to win victories that will eclipse all their past achievements.

The threefold task to which your attention is now directed comprises the proclamation, expansion and consolidation of the Faith. We urge you to concentrate your deliberations not only on the exchange of ideas for the prosecution of this task, but on ways and means for fostering collaboration among the Bahá'í Communities of Central and South America so that the most fruitful harvest may be gathered in all three aspects of the teaching work and enable you to achieve your remaining goals of the Nine Year Plan.

Our loving, ardent prayers will be offered at the Sacred Threshold, that the Almighty may inspire your discussions in this historic Conference and crown all your efforts with victory.

THE UNIVERSAL HOUSE OF JUSTICE

Riḍván Message 1972

Riḍván 1972

To the Bahá'ís of the World

Dearly-loved Friends,

The opening of the final year of the Nine Year Plan sees the Bahá'í world community poised for overwhelming victory. With grateful hearts we acknowledge the continuing confirmations which have attended its efforts and the Divine Bounties which have never ceased to rain down upon this blessed, this ever-developing embryonic world order.

The Mashriqu'l-Adhkár of Panama, the Mother Temple of Latin America, will be dedicated this Riḍván. Three beloved Hands of the Cause, Amatu'l-Bahá Rúḥíyyih Khánum representing the Universal House of Justice, Ugo Giachery and Dhikru'lláh Khádem will attend this historic ceremony. The imaginative and inspiring concept of the architect, Peter Tillotson, has been wonderfully realized and we extend to the National Spiritual Assembly of Panama on behalf of the entire Bahá'í world, loving congratulations on their achievement.

Although the dissolution of the National Spiritual Assembly of 'Iráq has, unhappily, resulted from the persecution of the Faith in that land, the thirteen new National Spiritual Assemblies which will come into being this Riḍván will bring the total number of these pillars of the Universal House of Justice to 113.

The goals requiring acquisition of properties and establishment of Teaching Institutes are well in hand and, in those countries where legal circumstances permit, incorporation of Assemblies and recognition of Bahá'í marriage and Holy Days are making good progress.

It is the teaching goals which must engage our attention and effort. Although more than 260 territories have achieved their assigned goals of localities where Bahá'ís reside, and in some cases have exceeded them, enabling the Bahá'í world community to rejoice in having outstripped on a world scale the total number of localities envisaged in the Plan, there are still some 60 territories where this goal is yet to be won and where its attainment must be given absolute priority between now and Riḍván 1973. It is expected that a large number of new Local Spiritual Assemblies will be established at Riḍván and immediately the position of this goal is ascertained a detailed listing of all territories throughout the world which have not yet won their goals for localities and Local Spiritual Assemblies will be sent to every National Spiritual Assembly for urgent release to the friends.

It is hoped that during this last year of the Plan the principle of collaboration between National Spiritual Assemblies will be extended far beyond the special tasks set in the Nine Year Plan. Those communities which have already attained their goals or are in clear sight of them should consider the world picture as disclosed by the listing mentioned above and do everything they can, without jeopardizing their own success, to assist their fellow communities with pioneers and traveling teachers, or in any other way possible. Such a process will greatly consolidate the unity and brotherhood of the Bahá'í world community.

In the meantime we call on all believers everywhere to prayerfully consider their personal circumstances, and to arise while there is yet time, to fill the international pioneer goals of the Plan. There are 267 pioneer needs still to be answered—75 in Africa, 57 in the Americas, 40 in Asia, 30 in Australasia and 65 in Europe.

The extraordinary advances made since that Riḍván of 1964

when the Nine Year Plan was begun, continuing the organized and purposeful process of teaching on a world scale instituted by our beloved Guardian when he launched the Ten Year Crusade, force upon our attention new requirements of this ever-growing world order both for its own organic life and in relation to the disintegrating world society in which it is set. The divergence between the ways of the world and of the Cause of God becomes ever wider. And yet the two must come together. The Bahá'í community must demonstrate in ever-increasing measure its ability to redeem the disorderliness, the lack of cohesion, the permissiveness, the godlessness of modern society; the laws, the religious obligations, the observances of Bahá'í life, Bahá'í moral principles and standards of dignity, decency and reverence, must become deeply implanted in Bahá'í consciousness and increasingly inform and characterize this community. Such a process will require a great development in the maturity and effectiveness of Local Spiritual Assemblies. The purposes and standards of the Cause must be more and more understood and courageously upheld. The influence of the Continental Boards of Counselors and the work of their Auxiliary Boards must develop and spread through the entire fabric of the Bahá'í community. A vast systematic program for the production of Bahá'í literature must be promoted.

Our immediate and inescapable task, however, is to ensure that every attainable goal of the Nine Year Plan is achieved. This must be done at all costs. No sacrifice, no deferment of cherished plans must be refused in order to discharge this "most important" of the many "important" duties facing us. Who can doubt that one last supreme effort will be crowned with success? Even now the national community to bear the laurels of first achieving every task assigned to it, Fiji, leads the procession of rejoicing and victorious communities within the

Army of Light. We may well emulate Bahá'í youth whose recent surge forward into the van of proclamation and teaching is one of the most encouraging and significant trends in the Faith, and who storm the gates of heaven for support in their enterprises by long-sustained, precedent and continuing prayer. We are all able to call upon Bahá'u'lláh for His Divine, all-powerful aid, and He will surely help us. For He is the Hearer of prayers, the Answerer.

THE UNIVERSAL HOUSE OF JUSTICE

Elucidation of the Nature of the Continental Boards of Counselors

24 April 1972

To the Continental Boards of Counselors
and National Spiritual Assemblies

Beloved Friends,

Recently we have received queries from several sources about the nature of the Institution of the Continental Boards of Counselors and its relationship to the Institution of the Hands of the Cause, and we feel it is timely for us to give further elucidation.

As with so many aspects of the Administrative Order, understanding of this subject will develop and clarify with the passage of time as that Order grows organically in response to the power and guidance of Almighty God and in accordance with the needs of a rapidly developing worldwide community. However, certain aspects are already so clear as to require a proper understanding by the friends.

In the Kitáb-i-'Ahdí (the Book of His Covenant) Bahá'u'lláh wrote "Blessed are the rulers and the learned in Al-Bahá," and referring to this very passage the beloved Guardian wrote on 4 November 1931:

> In this holy cycle the "learned" are, on the one hand, the Hands of the Cause of God, and, on the other, the teachers and diffusers of His teachings who do not rank as Hands, but who have attained an eminent position in the teaching work. As to the "rulers" they refer to the members of the Local, National and International Houses of Justice. The duties of each of these souls will be determined in the future. (Translated from the Persian).

The Hands of the Cause of God, the Counselors and the members of the Auxiliary Boards fall within the definition of the "learned" given by the beloved Guardian. Thus they are all intimately interrelated and it is not incorrect to refer to the three ranks collectively as one institution.

However, each is also a separate institution in itself. The Institution of the Hands of the Cause of God was brought into existence in the time of Bahá'u'lláh and when the Administrative Order was proclaimed and formally established by 'Abdu'l-Bahá in His Will, it became an auxiliary institution of the Guardianship. The Auxiliary Boards, in their turn, were brought into being by Shoghi Effendi as an auxiliary institution of the Hands of the Cause.

When, following the passing of Shoghi Effendi, the Universal House of Justice decided that it could not legislate to make possible the appointment of further Hands of the Cause, it became necessary for it to create a new institution, appointed by itself, to extend into the future the functions of protection and propagation vested in the Hands of the Cause and, with that in view, so to develop the Institution of the Hands that it could nurture the new institution and function in close collaboration with it as long as possible. It was also vital so to arrange matters as to make the most effective use of the unique services of the Hands themselves.

The first step in this development was taken in November 1964 when the Universal House of Justice formally related the Institution of the Hands to itself by stating that "Responsibility for decisions on matters of general policy affecting the institution of the Hands of the Cause, which was formerly exercised by the beloved Guardian, now devolves upon the Universal House of Justice as the supreme and central Institution of the Faith to which all must turn." At that time the number of members of the Auxiliary Boards was increased from 72 to 135, and the Hands of the Cause in each continent were called upon to appoint one or more members of their Auxiliary Boards to act in an executive capacity on behalf of and in the name of each Hand, thereby assisting him in carrying out his work.

In June 1968 the Institution of the Continental Boards of Counselors was brought into being, fulfilling the goal of extending the aforementioned functions of the Hands into the future, and this momentous decision was accompanied by the next step in the development of the Institution of the Hands of the Cause: the continental Hands were to serve henceforth on a worldwide basis and operate individually in direct relationship to the Universal House of Justice; the Hands ceased to be responsible for the direction of the Auxiliary Boards, which became an auxiliary institution of the Continental Boards of Counselors; the Hands of the Cause residing in the Holy Land were given the task of acting as liaison between the Universal House of Justice and the Boards of Counselors; and the working interrelationships between the Hands and the Boards of Counselors were established. Reference was also made to the future establishment by the Universal House of Justice, with the assistance of the Hands residing in the Holy Land, of an international teaching center in the Holy Land.

In July 1969 and at Riḍván 1970 further increases in the numbers of Counselors and Auxiliary Board members were made.

Other developments in the Institution of the Hands of the Cause and the Institution of the Continental Boards of Counselors will no doubt take place in future as the international teaching center comes into being and as the work of the Counselors expands.

We have noted that the Hands, the Counselors and the Auxiliary Boards are sometimes referred to by the friends as the "appointive arm" of the Administrative Order in contradistinction to the Universal House of Justice and the National and Local Assemblies which constitute the "elective arm." While there is truth in this description as it applies to the method used in the creation of these institutions, the friends should understand that it is not only the fact of appointment that particularly distinguishes the institutions of the Hands, Counselors and Auxiliary Boards. There are, for instance, many more believers appointed to committees in the "elective arm" than are serving in the so-called "appointive arm." A more striking distinction is that whereas the "rulers" in the Cause function as corporate bodies, the "learned" operate primarily as individuals.

In a letter written on 14 March 1927 to the Spiritual Assembly of the Bahá'ís of Istanbul, the Guardian's Secretary explained, on his behalf, the principle in the Cause of action by majority vote. He pointed out how, in the past, it was certain individuals who "accounted themselves as superior in knowledge and elevated in position" who caused division, and that it was those "who pretended to be the most distinguished of all" who "always proved themselves to be the source of contention." "But praise be to God," he continued, "that the Pen of Glory has done away with the unyielding and dictatorial views of the learned and the wise, dismissed the assertions of individuals as an authoritative criterion, even though they were recognized as the most accomplished and learned among men and ordained that all matters be referred to authorized centers and specified assemblies. Even so, no assembly has been invested with the absolute authority to deal with such general matters as affect the interests of nations. Nay rather, He has brought all the assemblies together under the shadow of one House of Justice, one divinely-appointed Center, so that there would be only one Center and all the rest integrated into a single body, revolving around one expressly-designated Pivot, thus making them all proof against schism and division." (Translated from the Persian).

Having permanently excluded the evils admittedly inherent in the institutions of the "learned" in past dispensations, Bahá'u'lláh has nevertheless embodied in His Administrative Order the beneficent elements which exist in such institutions, elements which are of fundamental value for the progress of the Cause, as can be gauged from even a cursory reading of the Guardian's message of 4 June 1957.

The existence of institutions of such exalted rank, comprising individuals who play such a vital role, who yet have no legislative, administrative or judicial authority, and are entirely devoid of priestly functions or the right to make authoritative interpretations, is a feature of Bahá'í administration unparalleled in the religions of the past. The newness and uniqueness of this concept make it difficult to grasp; only as the Bahá'í Community grows and the believers are increasingly able to contemplate its administrative structure uninfluenced by concepts from past ages, will the vital interdependence of the "rulers" and "learned" in the Faith be properly understood, and the inestimable value of their interaction be fully recognized.

With loving Bahá'í greetings,
THE UNIVERSAL HOUSE OF JUSTICE

Message to Bahá'í Unity Conference— Ganado, Arizona

18 May 1972

Bahá'í Unity Conference
Ganado, Arizona

Beloved Friends,

Praise be to the Almighty that you have gathered in that beautiful spot in a spirit of love and harmony for the purpose of strengthening the bonds of unity between yourselves and among all men.

The All-Wise Creator of earth and heaven has from the beginning which has no beginning sent to His peoples Divine Messengers to guide them to the Straight Path. These Wise Ones have come to establish the unity of the Kingdom in human hearts. This great evolutionary process of building the organic unity of the human race has entered a new stage with this mighty message of Bahá'u'lláh. His voice is the voice of the Great Spirit. His love for human kind is the force of the New Age.

He who sends the rain, who causes the sun and the stars to shine, the rivers to flow, the winds to blow and the earth to give forth her bounties has in this Great Day sent to all mankind Bahá'u'lláh. It is this Great One who has opened the door of divine knowledge to every soul. It is His teachings that will establish world unity and bring about universal peace.

The people of the world are the tools in His hand. They must strive to understand His message and to walk in the path of His divine guidance. Every human being is responsible in this day to seek the truth for himself and thereafter to live according to that wise counsel. The old ones have all longed for this sweet message. Praise God that you have found it.

Now awakened to new wisdom, now guided to the straight path, now illumined with this mighty message, strive you day and night to guide and assist the thirsty ones in all lands to the ever-flowing fountain, the wandering ones to this fortress of certainty, the ignorant ones to this source of knowledge and the seekers to that One for whom their hearts long.

May your consultation reach so high a level of endeavor and purpose that the Great One will open before your faces the doors of the paradise of wisdom and love and cause the light of the Abhá Beauty to shine in your midst.

With loving Bahá'í greetings,
THE UNIVERSAL HOUSE OF JUSTICE

Establishment of Local Spiritual Assemblies during the Final Year of the Nine Year Plan

28 May 1972

To: All National Spiritual Assemblies

Dear Bahá'í Friends,

In order to stimulate the teaching work in every land and encourage the friends during this last year of the Nine Year Plan we have decided that as soon as the number of adult believers in any locality reaches or exceeds nine they are permitted to form their Local Spiritual Assembly immediately, rather than wait until 21 April 1973.

We hope moreover that, especially in the areas where the people are entering the Cause in troops, the implementation of this decision will increase the number of those communities which will, without the need for outside assistance, reelect their Assemblies on the first day of Riḍván in 1973 and in succeeding years.

It is our prayer at the Sacred Threshold that during the months ahead the steadily mounting number of these divine institutions will tremendously reinforce the labors of the valiant servants of the Blessed Beauty in every clime.

With loving Bahá'í greetings,
THE UNIVERSAL HOUSE OF JUSTICE

Announcement of the Decision to Build the Seat of The Universal House of Justice

7 June 1972

To: All National Spiritual Assemblies

Dear Bahá'í Friends,

With great joy we send you the following message, couched in cable form, and ask you to share it with all the friends in your jurisdiction. The text has been cabled to "Bahá'í News" for publication in its next issue.

Joyfully inform Bahá'í world range and acceleration growth Cause Bahá'u'lláh local national levels and resultant expansion activities World Center impel us now announce ere completion Nine Year Plan decision initiate procedure select architect design building for seat Universal House Justice envisaged beloved Guardian on far flung arc heart Mount Carmel centering spot consecrated resting places sister brother mother beloved Master. Construction this center legislation God's world redeeming Order will constitute first major step development area surrounding Holy Shrine since completion International Archives Building. Moved pay tribute express heartfelt gratitude outstanding services Robert McLaughlin in preparation for this historic undertaking. Fervently praying project now initiated may during years immediately ahead progress uninterruptedly speedily attain majestic consummation.

With loving Bahá'í greetings,
THE UNIVERSAL HOUSE OF JUSTICE

Exhortation to Blot Out
Every Last Trace of Prejudice

13 July 1972

To: All National Spiritual Assemblies

Dear Bahá'í Friends,

The blessings of the Ancient Beauty are being showered upon the followers of the Greatest Name. Our efforts to serve Him and humanity are being crowned with victories through- out the world. As we give thanks for these splendid achieve- ments, as the Cause of God spreads in every land, as our institutions become more perfected, as the number of believ- ers increases over the face of the planet, our individual lives must increasingly mirror forth each day the teachings of Bahá'u'lláh and we must so live our lives that all will see in us a different people. The acts we perform, the attitudes we man- ifest, the very words we speak should be an attraction, a magnet, drawing the sincere to the Divine Teachings.

Bahá'u'lláh tells us that prejudice in its various forms de- stroys the edifice of humanity. We are adjured by the Divine Messenger to eliminate all forms of prejudice from our lives. Our outer lives must show forth our beliefs. The world must see that, regardless of each passing whim or current fashion of the generality of mankind, the Bahá'í lives his life according to the tenets of his Faith. We must not allow the fear of rejection by our friends and neighbors to deter us from our goal: to live the Bahá'í life. Let us strive to blot out from our lives every last trace of prejudice—racial, religious, political, economic, national, tribal, class, cultural, and that which is based on differences of education or age. We shall be distinguished from our non-Bahá'í associates if our lives are adorned with this principle.

If we allow prejudice of any kind to manifest itself in us, we shall be guilty before God of causing a setback to the progress and real growth of the Faith of Bahá'u'lláh. It is incumbent upon every believer to endeavor with a fierce determination to eliminate this defect from his thoughts and acts. It is the duty of the institutions of the Faith to inculcate this principle in the hearts of the friends through every means at their disposal including summer schools, conferences, institutes and study classes.

The fundamental purpose of the Faith of Bahá'u'lláh is the realization of the organic unity of the entire human race. Bearing this glorious destiny in mind, and with entire reliance on the promises of the Blessed Beauty, we should follow His exhortation:

> We love to see you at all times consorting in amity and concord within the paradise of My good-pleasure, and to inhale from your acts the fragrance of friendliness and unity, of loving-kindness and fellowship.

With loving Bahá'í greetings,
THE UNIVERSAL HOUSE OF JUSTICE

Sacrifice of Three Iranian Bahá'í Students in the Philippine Islands

19 September 1972

To the Bahá'ís of the World

With feelings of deep sorrow we relate to the Bahá'í world the distressing circumstances surrounding the murder of three

Iranian Bahá'í students, pioneers to the Philippine Islands.

Parvíz Sádiqí, Farámarz Vujdání and Parvíz Furúghí were among a number of Iranian Bahá'í youth who answered the call for pioneers. With eleven others they registered at the Universities in Mindanao with the intention of completing their studies and proclaiming the Faith of Bahá'u'lláh. These three had conceived the plan of making teaching trips to a rural area inhabited by Muslims. When on July 31st the authorities of Mindanao State University were notified that they had left the campus the previous day and had not yet returned, search parties were immediately formed and the assistance of the police and local authorities obtained. After inquiries and search, led entirely by President Tamano of Mindanao State University, the bodies of the three young men were found in a shallow grave. They had been shot, grievously mutilated and two had been decapitated. The bodies were removed and given Bahá'í burial in a beautiful plot donated for the purpose.

Immediately upon receipt of the tragic news, Vicente Samaniego, Counselor in Northeast Asia, in close cooperation with the National Spiritual Assembly of the Philippines, acted vigorously on behalf of the Bahá'ís and was given the utmost cooperation and sympathy by the authorities, police, military and civil. A convocation was called, attended by more than 900 students, faculty members and University officials. Prayers were said in English, Arabic and Persian. The President of the University gave a talk in which he said that the murdered Iranian students are not ordinary students, for with them is the Message of Bahá'u'lláh which is the way to unity. The Council of the Student Body asked that their new Social Hall be renamed Iranian Student Memorial Hall. Three thousand people marched in the funeral procession and six hundred went to the burial site to attend the interment.

A dignified burial was conducted by the Bahá'ís in the presence of University authorities and friends.

The relatives and friends of these three young men, who gave their lives in the service of the Blessed Beauty, are assured of the loving sympathy and prayers of their fellow believers. The sacrifice made by these youth adds a crown of glory to the wonderful services now being performed by Bahá'í youth throughout the world. Bahá'u'lláh Himself testifies:

> They that have forsaken their country in the path of God and subsequently ascended unto His presence, such souls shall be blessed by the Concourse on High and their names recorded by the Pen of Glory among such as have laid down their lives as martyrs in the path of God, the Help in Peril, the Self-Subsistent.

The Universal House of Justice

Adoption of the Constitution of The Universal House of Justice

26 November 1972

To All National Spiritual Assemblies

Dear Bahá'í Friends,

The following cable has just been sent to the United States "Bahá'í News" for publication.

> With grateful joyous hearts announce entire Bahá'í world adoption profoundly significant step in unfoldment mission supreme organ Bahá'í world commonwealth through formulation constitution Universal House Justice. After offering humble prayers gratitude on Day Covenant at three Sacred Thresholds Bahjí Haifa members gathered council chamber precincts house blessed Master appended their signatures fixed seal on instrument envisaged writings beloved Guardian hailed by him as Most Great Law Faith Bahá'u'lláh. Fully assured measure just taken will further

reinforce ties binding World Center to national local communities throughout world release fresh energies increase enthusiasm confidence valiant workers His divine vineyard laboring assiduously bring mankind under shelter His all glorious Covenant.

Please share this joyous news with the friends. It is anticipated that the Constitution will be published at Riḍván.

> With loving Bahá'í greetings,
> THE UNIVERSAL HOUSE OF JUSTICE

Activities for the Year Preceding the Global Plan to Be Launched Riḍván 1974

14 January 1973

To: All National Spiritual Assemblies

Dear Bahá'í Friends,

As the Bahá'í world approaches the triumphant conclusion of the Nine Year Plan it gives us the utmost gratification to see that a few National Spiritual Assemblies have already formulated plans for activity during the coming Bahá'í year.

The next global plan will be launched at Riḍván 1974 and you will therefore have twelve months to prepare for it. We call upon you all to take the greatest possible advantage of that year to:

Strengthen the foundations of your achievements through developing and enriching Bahá'í community life, fostering youth activity and through all means suited to your circumstances; and

Continue expansion of the Faith, trying new openings and possibilities not fully explored when you were under the pressure of other priorities.

Obviously conditions differ in the various areas under the jurisdiction of the National Spiritual Assemblies, and the goals which each Assembly adopts must be suited to its particular circumstances and possibilities, but, as the beloved Guardian once pointed out, "The broader the basis" of such a campaign, and "the deeper its roots, the finer the flower into which it shall eventually blossom."

We ask you to make your plans now and to send us your report of them to reach us as soon as possible and not later than 1st April 1973 so that we may present a consolidated summary to the International Convention. We feel that such a summary will be an inspiration and a source of new ideas to the delegates when they are consulting upon the challenges that lie before the Bahá'í community in the years ahead and which must be faced during the next global plan. Moreover, the achievements of the coming year, added to the great victories of the Nine Year Plan, will enable the worldwide Bahá'í community to enter with even greater assurance upon the next stage of its ever-unfolding destiny.

We pray at the Holy Shrines that the blessings of Bahá'u'lláh may guide and assist you with a fresh measure of His divine grace in the few months separating us from the glorious festivities of next Riḍván.

With loving Bahá'í greetings,
THE UNIVERSAL HOUSE OF JUSTICE

Announcement of the Completion of the Synopsis and Codification of the Kitáb-i-Aqdas

19 January 1973

To: All National Spiritual Assemblies

Dear Bahá'í Friends,

The following cable has just been sent to the United States "Bahá'í News" for publication:

Joyfully announce completion synopsis codification Kitáb-i-Aqdas for publication Riḍván synchronizing celebration hundredth anniversary revelation Most Holy Book fulfilling World Center goal Nine Year Plan. Confident release this publication envisaged by beloved Guardian and whose main features he outlined will constitute another significant step path leading Bahá'í community full maturity establishment World Order Bahá'u'lláh.

Please share this joyous news with the friends.

With loving Bahá'í greetings,
THE UNIVERSAL HOUSE OF JUSTICE

Challenge to Individuals to Obey the Law of God in Their Personal Lives

6 February 1973

To All National Spiritual Assemblies

Dear Bahá'í Friends,

The following is an excerpt from a letter written recently in response to questions from an individual believer. As it is of general interest we are sending it to you so that you may share it with the friends within your jurisdiction in whatever manner you judge wise and necessary.

Just as there are laws governing our physical lives, requiring that we must supply our bodies with certain foods, maintain them within a certain range of temperatures, and so forth, if we wish to avoid physical disabilities, so also there are laws governing our spiritual lives. These laws are revealed to mankind in each age by the Manifestation of God, and obedience to them is of vital importance if each human being, and mankind in general, is to develop properly and harmoniously. Moreover, these various aspects are interdependent. If an individual violates the spiritual laws for his own development he will cause injury not only to himself but to the society in which he lives. Similarly, the condition of society has a direct effect on the individuals who must live within it.

As you point out, it is particularly difficult to follow the laws of Bahá'u'lláh in present-day society whose accepted practice is so at variance with the standards of the Faith. However, there are certain laws that are so fundamental to the healthy functioning of human society that they must be upheld whatever the circumstances. Realizing the degree of human frailty, Bahá'u'lláh has provided that other laws are to be applied only gradually, but these too, once they are applied, must be followed, or else society will not be re-formed but will sink into an ever worsening condition. It is the challenging task of the Bahá'ís to obey the law of God in their own lives, and gradually to win the rest of mankind to its acceptance.

In considering the effect of obedience to the laws on individual lives, one must remember that the purpose of this life is to prepare the soul for the next. Here one must learn to control and direct one's animal impulses, not to be a slave to them. Life in this world is a succession of tests and achievements, of falling short and of making new spiritual advances. Sometimes the course may seem very hard, but one can witness, again and again, that the soul who stead-fastly obeys the law of Bahá'u'lláh, however hard it may seem, grows spiritually, while the one who compromises with the law for the sake of his own apparent happiness is seen to have been following a chimera: he does not attain the happiness he sought, he retards his spiritual advance and often brings new problems upon himself.

To give one very obvious example: the Bahá'í law requiring consent of parents to marriage. All too often nowadays such consent is withheld by non-Bahá'í parents for reasons of bigotry or racial prejudice; yet we have seen again and again the profound effect on those very parents of the firmness of the children in the Bahá'í law, to the extent that not only is the consent ultimately given in many cases, but the character of the parents can be affected and their relationship with their child greatly strengthened.

Thus, by upholding Bahá'í law in the face of all difficulties we not only strengthen our own characters but influence those around us.

The Bahá'í teaching on sexual intercourse is very clear. It is permissible only between a man and the woman who is his wife. In this connection we share with you extracts from four letters written on behalf of the Guardian which throw light on various aspects of the matter. One of them contains the paragraph that you quote in your letter.

With reference to the question you have asked concerning the Bahá'í attitude towards the problem of sex and its relation to marriage.

The Bahá'í Teachings on this matter, which is of such vital concern and about which there is such a wide divergency of views, are very clear and emphatic. Briefly stated the Bahá'í conception of sex is based on the belief that chastity should be strictly practiced by both sexes, not only because it is in itself highly commendable ethically, but also due to its being the only way to a happy and successful marital life. Sex relationships of any form, outside marriage, are not permissible therefore, and whoso violates this rule will not only be responsible to God, but will incur the necessary punishment from society.

The Bahá'í Faith recognizes the value of the sex impulse, but condemns its illegitimate and improper expressions such as free love, companionate marriage and others, all of which it considers positively harmful to man and to the society in which he lives. The proper use of the sex instinct is the natural right of every individual, and it is precisely for this very purpose that the institution of marriage has been established. The Bahá'ís do not believe in the suppression of the sex impulse but in its regulation and control.

(From a letter dated September 5, 1938,
to an individual believer)

The question you raise as to the place in one's life that a deep bond of love with someone we meet other than our husband or wife can have is easily defined in view of the teachings. Chastity implies both before and after marriage an unsullied, chaste sex life. Before marriage absolutely chaste, after marriage absolutely faithful to one's chosen companion. Faithful in all sexual acts, faithful in word and in deed.

The world today is submerged, amongst other things, in an over-exaggeration of the importance of physical love, and a dearth of spiritual values. In as far as possible the believers should try to realize this and rise above the level of their fellowmen who are, typical of all decadent periods in history, placing so much overemphasis on the purely physical side of mating. Outside of their normal, legitimate married life they should seek to establish bonds of comradeship and love which are eternal and founded on the spiritual life of man, not on his physical life. This is one of the many fields in which it is incumbent on the Bahá'ís to set the example and lead the way to a true human standard of life, when the soul of man is exalted and his body but the tool for his enlightened spirit. Needless to say this does not preclude the living of a perfectly normal sex life in its legitimate channel of marriage.

> (From a letter dated September 28, 1941, to an individual believer)

Concerning your question whether there are any legitimate forms of expression of the sex instinct outside of marriage; according to the Bahá'í Teachings no sexual act can be considered lawful unless performed between lawfully married persons. Outside of marital life there can be no lawful or healthy use of the sex impulse. The Bahá'í youth should, on the one hand, be taught the lesson of self-control which, when exercised, undoubtedly has a salutary effect on the development of character and of personality in general, and on the other should be advised, nay even encouraged, to contract marriage while still young and in full possession of their physical vigor. Economic factors, no doubt, are often a serious hindrance to early marriage but in most cases are only an excuse, and as such should not be over stressed.

> (From a letter dated December 13, 1940, to an individual believer)

As regards your question whether it would be advisable and useful for you to marry again; he feels unable to give you any definite answer on that point, as this is essentially a private affair about which you, and the friends around you or your local assembly are in a much better position to judge. Of course, under normal circumstances, every person should consider it his moral duty to marry. And this is what Bahá'u'lláh has encouraged the believers to do. But marriage is by no means an obligation. In the last

resort it is for the individual to decide whether he wishes
to lead a family life or live in a state of celibacy.

(From a letter dated May 3, 1936,
to an individual believer)

You express surprise at the Guardian's reference to "the
necessary punishment from society." In the Kitáb-i-Aqdas
Bahá'u'lláh prohibits sexual immorality and in the Annex
to that Book states that the various degrees of sexual offenses
and the punishments for them are to be decided by the
Universal House of Justice. In this connection it should be
realized that there is a distinction drawn in the Faith between the attitudes which should characterize individuals
in their relationship to other people, namely, loving for-
giveness, forbearance, and concern with one's own sins, not
the sins of others, and those attitudes which should be
shown by the Spiritual Assemblies, whose duty is to administer the law of God with justice.

A number of sexual problems, such as homosexuality
and transsexuality can well have medical aspects, and in
such cases recourse should certainly be had to the best
medical assistance. But it is clear from the teaching of
Bahá'u'lláh that homosexuality is not a condition to which
a person should be reconciled, but is a distortion of his or
her nature which should be controlled and overcome. This
may require a hard struggle, but so also can be the struggle
of a heterosexual person to control his or her desires. The
exercise of self-control in this, as in so very many other
aspects of life, has a beneficial effect on the progress of the
soul. It should, moreover, be borne in mind that although
to be married is highly desirable, and Bahá'u'lláh has
strongly recommended it, it is not the central purpose of
life. If a person has to wait a considerable period before

finding a spouse, or if ultimately, he or she must remain single, it does not mean that he or she is thereby unable to fulfill his or her life's purpose.

In all this we have been speaking about the attitude that Bahá'ís should have towards the law of Bahá'u'lláh. You, however, as a doctor working mainly as a counselor in family and sexual problems, will mostly be concerned with advising non-Bahá'ís who do not accept, and see no reason to follow, the laws of Bahá'u'lláh. You are already a qualified practitioner in your field, and no doubt you give advice on the basis of what you have learned from study and experience—a whole fabric of concepts about the human mind, its growth, development and proper functioning, which you have learned and evolved without reference to the teachings of Bahá'u'lláh. Now, as a Bahá'í, you know that what Bahá'u'lláh teaches about the purpose of human life, the nature of the human being and the proper conduct of human lives, is divinely revealed and therefore true. However, it will inevitably take time for you not only to study the Bahá'í teachings so that you clearly understand them, but also to work out how they modify your professional concepts. This is, of course, not an unusual predicament for a scientist. How often in the course of research is a factor discovered which requires a revolution in thinking over a wide field of human endeavor. You must be guided in each case by your own professional knowledge and judgment as illuminated by your growing knowledge of the Bahá'í teachings; undoubtedly you will find that your own understanding of the human problems dealt with in your work will change and develop and you will see new and improved ways of helping the people who come to you. Psychology is still a very young and inexact science, and as the years go by Bahá'í psychologists, who know from the teachings of Bahá'u'lláh the true pattern of human life, will be able to make great strides in the development of this science, and will help profoundly in the alleviation of human suffering.

With loving Bahá'í greetings,
THE UNIVERSAL HOUSE OF JUSTICE

Purchase of Mazra'ih Mansion

15 March 1973

To All National Spiritual Assemblies

Dear Bahá'í Friends,

The following cable has just been sent to the United States "Bahá'í News" for publication.

Occasion Naw-Rúz 130 joyously announce Bahá'í world acquisition by purchase mansion Mazra'ih result several years patient persistent determined negotiations thereby adding to Bahá'í endowments Holy Land first residence Bahá'u'lláh after nine years spent walled prison city 'Akká. Control this holy site reacquired by beloved Guardian after lapse more than fifty years when he secured lease mansion 1950 extended to present time. Purchase includes land area approximating twentyfour thousand square meters highly suitable extension gardens cultivation. Offering prayer thanksgiving Sacred Threshold this greatly cherished bounty.

Please share this joyous news with the friends.

With loving Bahá'í greetings,
THE UNIVERSAL HOUSE OF JUSTICE

Riḍván Message 1973

Riḍván 1973

To the Bahá'ís of the World

Dearly-loved Friends,

We announce with joyful and thankful hearts the completion in overwhelming victory of the world-encircling Nine Year Plan. The Army of Light has won its second global campaign; it has surpassed the goals set for expansion and has achieved a truly impressive degree of universal participation, the twin objectives of the Plan. With gratitude and love we testify to the unceasing confirmations which Bahá'u'lláh has showered upon His servants, enabling each and every one of us to offer Him some part of the labor, the devotion, the sacrifice, the supplication which He has so bountifully rewarded. At this Centenary of the Revelation of the Most Holy Book, the Community of the Most Great Name lays its tribute of victory at His feet, acknowledging that it is He Who has bestowed it.

The Cause of God at the end of the Nine Year Plan is immensely more widespread, more firmly founded, and its own international relations more closely knit than in 1964 when the Plan was launched. Ninety-five new territories have been opened to the Faith; the 69 National Spiritual Assemblies which shouldered the world community's task have become 113, 5 more than called for. These embryonic secondary Houses of Justice are supported by more than 17,000 Local Spiritual Assemblies, 3,000 in excess of the goal and 12,000 more than at the beginning of the Plan. Bahá'ís reside in 69,500 localities, 15,000 more than called for, and 54,000 more than in 1964. Bahá'í literature has been translated into 225 more languages bringing the total number to 571; 63

Temple sites, 56 National Ḥaẓíratu'l-Quds, and 62 National Endowments have been acquired bringing the total numbers of these properties to 98, 112 and 104 respectively; 50 Teaching Institutes and Summer and Winter Schools are playing their part in Bahá'í education and 15 Publishing Trusts produce Bahá'í literature in major languages of the world. The Mother Temple of Latin America has been built and dedicated. Among those goals whose achievement is dependent on favorable circumstances outside our control are the incorporation of Assemblies and recognition of Bahá'í Holy Days. It is gratifying to record that 90 National Spiritual Assemblies and 1,556 Local Spiritual Assemblies—181 more·than the total number called for—are incorporated, while Bahá'í Holy Days are recognized in 64 countries and Bahá'í certification of marriage in 40.

This great expansion of the Faith required an army of international pioneers. Two major calls were raised, for 461 and 733, which together with others for particular posts made an overall total of 1,344. The Community of the Most Great Name responded with 3,553 who actually left their homes, 2,265 of whom are still at their posts.

At the World Center of the Faith the collation and classification of the Bahá'í Sacred Scriptures and of the writings of Shoghi Effendi have been carried forward in ever increasing volume, a task supported and enriched by the labors of a special committee appointed by the Persian National Spiritual Assembly. The material at the World Center includes some 2,600 original Tablets by Bahá'u'lláh, 6,000 by 'Abdu'l-Bahá and 2,300 letters of Shoghi Effendi. There are in addition some 18,000 authenticated copies of other such Tablets and letters. All these have been studied, important passages from them excerpted and classified, and the subject matter indexed under 400 general headings.

A Synopsis and Codification of the Laws and Ordinances of

the Kitáb-i-Aqdas—completing the considerable progress made by the beloved Guardian in this task—is being published on the Centenary of the Revelation of the Most Holy Book, which, as already announced, is to be celebrated both in the Holy Land and throughout the Bahá'í world during this Ridván.

The Constitution of the Universal House of Justice, hailed by Shoghi Effendi as the Most Great Law of the Faith of Bahá'u'lláh, has been formulated and published.

The gardens in Bahjí and on Mount Carmel have been significantly extended and plans have been approved for the befitting development and beautification of the entire area of Bahá'í property surrounding the Holy Shrines in Bahjí and Haifa.

The worldwide proclamation of the Faith, an intensive and long-to-be-sustained process initiated during the third phase of the Plan, opened in October 1967 with the commemoration of the Centenary of Bahá'u'lláh's Proclamation to the kings and rulers which had centered around His revelation of the Súriy-i-Mulúk in Adrianople. This historic event was commemorated at six Intercontinental Conferences held simultaneously around the planet. A further nine Oceanic and Continental Conferences held during the Plan gave great impetus to this proclamation program. The fifteen Conferences were attended by nearly 17,000 believers and attracted great publicity by press and radio and were made the occasion of acquainting dignitaries and notabilities with the Divine Message. The presentation, on behalf of the Universal House of Justice, to 142 Heads of State, of a specially produced book containing the translation into English of the Tablets and passages of Scripture in which Bahá'u'lláh, some hundred years before, had issued His mighty Proclamation to mankind, initiated this campaign, which will continue long beyond the end of the Nine Year Plan.

The outstanding development in the relationship of the Bahá'í International Community to the United Nations was the accreditation of that Community as a nongovernmental organization with consultative status to the Economic and Social Council of the United Nations. The Bahá'í International Community now has a permanent representative at United Nations and maintains an office in New York.

The loved and revered Hands of the Cause have rendered sacrificial and distinguished service throughout the Nine Year Plan. They have, in all parts of the world, inspired the friends, assisted National Spiritual Assemblies, promoted the teaching work and played a vital part in the success of the Plan. The lagging fortunes of more than one national community have been revolutionized by a visit of a Hand of the Cause; swift and energetic action, inspired by the Hand, has been followed by astonishing results, completely reversing that community's prospects. They have added distinguished works to the literature of the Faith.

The goal of the Plan to develop "The institution of the Hands of the Cause of God, in consultation with the body of the Hands of the Cause, with a view to the extension into the future of its appointed functions of protection and propagation," was accomplished in stages, leading to the establishment of eleven Continental Boards of Counselors, whose members were appointed by the Universal House of Justice and who assumed responsibility for the Auxiliary Boards for protection and propagation. The beloved Hands no longer remained individually identified with any particular continent—except insofar as their residence was concerned —but extended their sphere of action to the whole planet. The Continental Boards of Counselors, advised and guided by the Hands of the Cause of God and working in close collaboration with them, have already, in their brief period of office, performed outstanding and distinguished services.

Three highly portentous developments have taken place during the Nine Year Plan, namely, the advance of youth to the forefront of the teaching work, a great increase in the financial resources of the Faith, and an astonishing proliferation of inter-National Assembly assistance projects.

The first, the heartwarming upsurge of Bahá'í youth, has changed the face of the teaching work; impenetrable barriers have been broken or overpassed by eager teams of young Bahá'ís, dedicated and prayerful, presenting the Divine Message in ways acceptable to their own generation from which it has spread and is spreading throughout the social structure. The entire Bahá'í world has been thrilled by this development. Having rejected the values and standards of the old world, Bahá'í youth are eager to learn and adapt themselves to the standards of Bahá'u'lláh and so to offer the Divine Program to fill the gap left by the abandonment of the old order.

The vast increase in the financial resources of the Faith called for under the Plan has evoked a heartwarming response from the entire Bahá'í community. Not only the Bahá'í International Fund but the local, national and continental Funds of the Faith have been sacrificially supported. This practical proof of the love which the friends bear for the Faith has enabled all the work to go forward—the support of pioneers and traveling teachers, the raising of Mashriqu'l-Adhkárs and acquisition of Bahá'í properties, the purchase of Holy Places in the Cradle of the Faith and at the World Center, the development of educational institutions and all the multifarious activities of a vigorous, onward-marching, constructive world community. It is of interest that sixty percent of the international funds of the Faith is used to assist the work of National Spiritual Assemblies, to promote the teaching work and to defend the Cause against attacks in many parts of the world. Without such help from the Bahá'í world community many National Assemblies would be paralyzed in their efforts of expansion and deepening. The administration of Ḥuqúqu'lláh has been strengthened in preparation for its extension to other parts of the world. An International Deputization Fund was established at the World Center to assist pioneers and traveling teachers who were ready to serve but unable to provide their own expenses, and this Fund was later extended to the support of projects on national homefronts. Contribution to the Fund is a service which will never cease to be open to all believers; the growth of the Faith and the rise of its Administrative Order require an ever-increasing outpouring of our substance, commensurate in however small a measure with the bounty and liberality of the outpouring confirmations of Bahá'u'lláh.

When the Plan was launched 219 assistance projects were specified whereby national communities would render financial, pioneering or teaching aid to others, generally remote from them geographically. The intention was to strengthen the bonds of unity between distant parts of the Bahá'í world with different social, cultural and historical backgrounds. At the end of the Plan more than 600 such projects had been carried out. Intercommunity cooperation has been further developed in the field of publishing Bahá'í literature, notably in Spanish and French and the languages of Africa. A vast field of fruitful endeavor lies open in this respect.

In some countries due to lack of freedom, to actual repression in others, to legal and physical obstacles in yet others, certain particular goals—mainly those requiring incorporation or recognition—could not be won. Foreseeing this, the Universal House of Justice called upon national communities in lands where there is freedom to practice and promote the Faith, to exceed their own goals and thus ensure that the overall goals would be won. It has proved still impossible to begin work on the erection of the Ma<u>sh</u>riqu'l-A<u>dh</u>kár in Ṭihrán, but contracts have been signed for the preparation of detailed drawings, geological surveys are being made, and everything made ready for immediate action whenever the situation in Persia becomes propitious.

During the period of the Nine Year Plan a number of important and interesting events, not directly associated with it, have taken place. First and foremost was the commemoration, in the precincts of the Qiblih of the Bahá'í world, of the centenary of the arrival at the prison-city of 'Akká, as foretold in former Scriptures, of the Promised One of all ages.

The Mansion of Mazra'ih, often referred to by the beloved Guardian as one of the "twin mansions" in which the Blessed Beauty resided after nine years within the walled prison-city of 'Akká, and dear to the hearts of the believers by reason of its associations with their Lord, has at last been purchased together with 24,000 square meters of land extending into the plain on its eastward side.

The raising of the obelisk, marking the site of the future Ma<u>sh</u>riqu'l-A<u>dh</u>kár on Mount Carmel, completes a project initiated by the beloved Guardian.

The decision has been made and announced to the Bahá'í world, and the initial steps have been taken for the erection on Mount Carmel, at a site on the Arc as purposed by Shoghi Effendi, of the building which shall serve as the Seat of the Universal House of Justice.

The progress of the Cause of God gathers increasing momentum and we may with confidence look forward to the day when this Community, in God's good time, shall have traversed the stages predicated for it by its Guardian, and shall have raised on this tormented planet the fair mansions of God's Own Kingdom wherein humanity may find surcease from its self-induced confusion and chaos and ruin, and the hatreds and violence of this time shall be transmuted into an abiding sense of world brotherhood and peace. All this shall be accomplished within the Covenant of the everlasting Father, the Covenant of Bahá'u'lláh.

THE UNIVERSAL HOUSE OF JUSTICE

Election of
The Universal House of Justice—May 1973

3 May 1973

To All National Spiritual Assemblies

Dear Bahá'í Friends,

The following cable has just been sent to the United States "Bahá'í News" for publication:

Newly elected members Universal House of Justice 'Ali Nakhjavání Hushmand Fatheázam Amoz Gibson Ian Semple David Hofman Charles Wolcott Borrah Kavelin David Ruhe Hugh Chance.

With loving Bahá'í greetings,
THE UNIVERSAL HOUSE OF JUSTICE

In Memoriam

The Hand of the Cause of God Hermann Grossmann

9 July 1968

To: All National Spiritual Assemblies

Dear Bahá'í Friends,

The following cable has been sent to the National Spiritual Assembly of Germany:

Deeply regret announce passing Hand Cause Hermann Grossmann. Greatly admired beloved Guardian his grievous loss deprives company Hands Cause outstanding collaborator and Bahá'í World Community staunch defender promoter Faith. His courageous loyalty during challenging years tests persecutions Germany outstanding services South America immortalized annals Faith. Invite all National Spiritual Assemblies hold memorial gatherings befitting his exalted rank exemplary services. Request those responsible Mother Temples arrange services auditorium.

Please share with all the friends.

With loving Bahá'í greetings,
THE UNIVERSAL HOUSE OF JUSTICE

Luṭfu'lláh Ḥakím

12 August 1968

To All National Spiritual Assemblies

Dear Bahá'í Friends,

We share with you the following cable which we have just sent to the National Spiritual Assembly of Persia:

Grieve announce passing Luṭfu'lláh Ḥakím dedicated servant Cause God. Special missions entrusted him full confidence reposed in him by Master and Guardian his close association with early distinguished believers East West including his collaboration Esslemont his services Persia British Isles Holy Land his membership appointed and elected International Bahá'í Council his election Universal House Justice will always be remembered immortal annals Faith Bahá'u'lláh. Inform believers hold befitting memorial meetings all centers. Convey all members his family expressions loving sympathy assurance prayers progress his radiant soul Abhá Kingdom.

In view of Dr. Ḥakím's long and devoted record of services to the Faith other National Spiritual Assemblies are requested to hold memorial gatherings. Special commemorative services should also be held in the four Mother Temples of the Bahá'í World.

> With loving Bahá'í greetings,
> THE UNIVERSAL HOUSE OF JUSTICE

The Hand of the Cause of God Ṭarázu'lláh Samandarí

4 September 1968

To All National Spiritual Assemblies

Dear Bahá'í Friends:

We have today sent the following cable to the National Assembly of Persia:

With sorrowful hearts announce passing Hand Cause God shield His Faith dearly loved Ṭarázu'lláh Samandarí ninety-third year his life on morrow commemoration centenary Bahá'u'lláh's arrival Holy Land. Faithful to last breath instructions his Lord his Master his Guardian he continued selfless devoted service unabated until falling ill during recent teaching mission. Unmindful illness he proceeded Holy Land participate centenary. Ever remembered hearts believers East West to whose lands he traveled bearing message his Lord whose communities he faithfully served this precious remnant Heroic Age who attained presence Blessed Beauty year His ascension now laid rest foot mountain God amidst throng believers assembled vicinity very spot Bahá'u'lláh first trod these sacred shores. Request all National Assemblies hold memorial services including four Mother Temples Bahá'í world befitting long life dedicated exemplary service Lord Hosts by one assured Center Covenant loving welcome presence Bahá'u'lláh Abhá Kingdom. Extend loving sympathy assurance prayers members distinguished family.

We request that memorial services be held as indicated.

With loving Bahá'í greetings,
THE UNIVERSAT HOUSE OF JUSTICE

Alvin Blum

24 September 1968

NatBahai
Honiara (British Solomon Islands)

Grieved learn passing Knight Bahá'u'lláh Alvin Blum steadfast devoted servant Faith his tireless labors pioneer Solomons unforgettable annals Bahá'í history praying Shrines progress soul Abhá Kingdom. Advise hold befitting memorial service Honiara. Requesting National Assembly Australia hold memorial service Mother Temple Antipodes. Convey loving sympathy members family.

UNIVERSAL HOUSE OF JUSTICE

Sara Kenny

24 September 1968

Bahá'í London SW 7
(England)

Grieved learn passing Knight Bahá'u'lláh Sara Kenny dedicated servant Cause native land stalwart pioneer Madeira whose devoted labors France membership first National Assembly and staunch defense Covenant contributed firm establishment foundation that national community. Assure family prayers Holy Shrines progress her soul Abhá Kingdom. Requesting National Assembly France hold befitting memorial service.

UNIVERSAL HOUSE OF JUSTICE

Maud Bosio

3 October 1968

Bahá'í
Rome

Deeply grieved learn passing devoted maidservant Bahá'u'lláh Maud Bosio early believer Italian community her sacrificial services success first Mediterranean Conference lovingly remembered praying Shrines progress her soul Abhá Kingdom advise hold befitting memorial gathering. Convey sympathy members family.

UNIVERSAL HOUSE OF JUSTICE

Nairn Forsythe Ward

9 June 1969

Bahá'í
Wilmette Illinois USA

Grieved announce sudden passing Nairn Forsythe Ward devoted believer who while enroute pioneer post Africa during

Crusade responded request Hands Cause remain Bahjí as custodian Sacred Shrine Blessed Beauty serving with wife Janet in that exalted post until his passing. His devoted services American homefront since early twenties long remembered. View his intimate association Geyserville advise holding befitting memorial service during summer school sessions there. Praying Shrines progress his soul Abhá Kingdom.

UNIVERSAL HOUSE OF JUSTICE

Ruth Randall Brown

4 November 1969

Bahá'í
Wilmette Illinois USA

Have today cabled NSA South Africa following quote grieved learn passing Ruth Randall Brown. Her long life devoted distinguished service Cause Bahá'u'lláh shining example all pioneers. Please arrange befitting memorial her behalf. Convey her family our loving sympathy assurance ardent prayers divine threshold progress her soul unquote.

UNIVERSAL HOUSE OF JUSTICE

The Hand of the Cause of God Agnes Alexander

4 January 1971

Bahá'í Faith
Honolulu Hawaiian Islands

Profoundly grieve passing illumined soul Hand Cause Agnes Alexander longstanding pillar Cause Far East first bring Faith Hawaiian Islands. Her long dedicated exemplary life service devotion Cause God anticipated by Center Covenant selecting her share May Maxwell imperishable honor mention Tablets Divine Plan. Her unrestrained unceasing pursuit teaching obedience command Bahá'u'lláh exhortations Master guidance beloved Guardian shining example all followers Faith. Her passing severs one more link Heroic Age. Assure family friends ardent prayers holiest shrine progress radiant soul request all National Spiritual Assemblies hold memorial meetings and those responsible hold service Mother Temples (Signed) Universal House of Justice

The Hand of the Cause of God Músá Banání

5 September 1971

Bahá'í Wilmette Illinois
(Wilmette, Illinois, USA)

Profoundly mourn passing dearly loved Hand Cause Músá Banání recall with deep affection his selfless unassuming prolonged services cradle Faith his exemplary pioneering Uganda culminating his appointment as Hand Cause Africa and praise beloved Guardian as spiritual conqueror that continent. Interment his remains African soil under shadow Mother Temple enhances spiritual luster that blessed spot. Fervently praying shrines progress his noble soul. May Africa now robbed staunch venerable promoter defender Faith follow his example cheer his heart Abhá Kingdom. Convey family most tender sympathies advise hold memorial meetings all communities Bahá'í world befitting gatherings Mother Temples.

UNIVERSAL HOUSE OF JUSTICE

Matthew Bullock

21 December 1972

Bahá'í
Wilmette Illinois USA

Grieve passing Knight Bahá'u'lláh Matthew Bullock distinguished promoter Faith convey family assurance prayers Holy

Threshold progress his soul advise hold memorial gathering Ma<u>sh</u>riqu'l-A<u>dh</u>kár.

UNIVERSAL HOUSE OF JUSTICE

Marion Little

12 March 1973

Bahá'í Wilmette
Wilmette Illinois USA

Have cabled National Assembly France quote ascension Abhá Kingdom Marion Little steadfast devoted servant Bahá'u'lláh more than fifty years teaching publishing pioneering United States South America Europe deprives American Bahá'í Community one its brightest ornaments Europe one most radiant pioneers. Her loyalty cheerfulness courage uplifted spirits friends assures bounteous reward. Offering prayers Sacred Threshold progress her soul recommend German National Assembly hold befitting memorial service Mother Temple Europe end quote please publish Bahá'í News.

UNIVERSAL HOUSE OF JUSTICE

Index

Index

'Abdu'l-Bahá: as Bahá'u'lláh's successor, 42; collation of Writings of, as goal of Nine Year Plan, 114; example of, 25; fiftieth anniversary of passing of, 68, 76-77; property surrounding teahouse of, acquired, 36; recording of voice of, must be used with restraint, 68; two charters provided by, 69; Will and Testament of, 38, 39, 43, 44, 69

Administrative Order: building of, is task of believers, 12; elective and appointive arms of, 94; establishment of Continental Boards of Counselors as further step in unfoldment of, 5, 8; role of learned and rulers in, 91-92, 94-95; unique feature of, 95

Afghanistan, 70, 83

Africa: problems of, 44-45, 48-49, 62; spiritual potential of believers in, 62-63; tribalism in, 45, 48-49; work of early pioneers in, 62

'Alá'í, Shu'á'u'lláh, 83

'Alá'í, Suhayl, 10

Alexander, Agnes, 70-71, 75, 78, 127-28

Americas, 73, 74

Appa, Seewoosumbur-Jeehoba, 9

Arabia, 70

Ardikání, Ḥusayn, 9

Arms, 26

Arnadóttir, Hólmfrídur, 80

Atlantic Ocean: historical importance of, 81; message of Oceanic Conference in North, 80-82

Auxiliary Boards, 90; as appointive arm of Administrative Order, 94; created by Shoghi Effendi, 92; duties of, 29-33; as learned, 92; membership of,

increased, 52-53, 93; relationship between, and Continental Boards of Counselors, 5, 7, 29-33, 92, 93, 116; relationship between, and Local and National Spiritual Assemblies, 29-33

Ayman, Iraj, 52

Bahá'í Community: contrast between, and present society, 12, 45, 49, 90; cooperation within, 118; developing and enriching, life, 103; universal participation will strengthen, 60; as worldwide, apolitical organization, 46. *See also* Believers

Bahá'u'lláh: collation of Writings of, as goal of Nine Year Plan, 114; commemoration of arrival of, in Holy Land, 14, 18, 21, 119; commemoration of centenary of proclamation of, 115; confinement of, in 'Akká, 10-11; Covenant of, 41-42, 120; voyage of, from Gallipoli to 'Akká, 10

Bahjí: extension of gardens of, 59, 84, 115; property adjacent to, acquired, 35-36

Baker, Dorothy, 13

Banání, Músá, 62, 128

Bangladesh. *See* East Pakistan

Believers: attitudes and conduct of, 34-35, 100, 110; duty of, to contribute to Fund, 17-18, 118; duty of, to live the life, 25, 62, 99-100; duty of, to teach, 17, 34, 35; fate of community depends on, 16, 29; importance of deepening new, 16; must set example for world, 45, 49, 108; relationship between, and society, 106; spiritual growth of, 106, 110; tasks of, 12, 46,

133